Greyhound S

Stories Of Rescued Greyhounds That Have Been Saved from Cruelty.

Compiled and Edited by Helen R. Etheridge

Published by Grey's Publishing

Published by Grey's Publishing,
4, Fifer's Lane,
Old Catton,
Norfolk.
England.
NR6 7AF
01603 423569

To order another copy of this book, please see the order form at the back of the book

Printed by Broadland Digital Ltd, Norwich

Picture on front cover: "Duke" by Maria Park
Picture on back cover: "Bella" by Sue Cole

I hope to do a second volume of greyhound stories so please send your rescued greyhound stories or comments about the book to **helenetheridge@btinternet.com**

50% of the profits from this book will be donated to Greyhound Action. To find out about their great campaigning work see **www.greyhoundaction.co.uk**

Contents

**This book is dedicated to Bonnie, Henry and George.
Words cannot express how much you are loved and missed still**

A Note From The Editor

I was sixteen when I first met a dog properly. She wasn't any old dog. She was Bella, a greyhound, who had been found by the side of the road, covered in mange and so skinny. She had been named Bella because, even in her terrible state, she still had a beautiful face. Several years later. when she was recovered, it was this face and her wonderful character, which enchanted me. Her coat is the softest coat you can imagine. She is so kind, and sensitive. She is intuitive and knows when something is wrong. It was her face looking back at me when I met Piglet, the first greyhound that I could ever call truly mine. It is thanks to her that my love of greyhounds developed into a passionate drive to help them, as best I can. It is also thanks to her that there is nowhere to sit where I live, as seven dogs take up all the seats!

As I write this, I can understand how all the contributors to this book must have felt writing their dog's story. One sits down with the intention of telling the history of their dog, but gets carried away with the emotion of their pure, uncomplicated love for the animals that share their lives. In this book there are stories of real cruelty that make uncomfortable reading, but the love and compassion of the writers proves that, eventually, these dogs were loved. I am not going to apologise for us all thinking that our dogs are the best dogs ever. If you have ever had the privilege of loving one of these wonderful greyhounds you will understand.

I am hoping to do another volume of this book, so do please send me your contributions. You never know; it may be your story that inspires someone to re-home a greyhound.

Helen Etheridge, 2006

Foreword by Twiggy

I am a huge admirer of *The Retired Greyhound Trust* and other charities that campaign on behalf of greyhounds, such as *Greyhound Action*, but I have to admit I didn't know a lot about it until a couple a years ago. I had taken my cat to the vet for her annual check up and on the message board a flyer caught my notice: "Please Help Gracie and Joe". Intrigued, I read on about these two ten year old greyhounds, who had been abandoned by their owner who was moving abroad. So *The Retired Greyhound Trust* had taken them in and was trying to re-home them. It also said the dogs wondered what they had done wrong. The difficulty was that they were two ten - year old dogs and they had to stay together. I called The Trust to see if I could help. I couldn't take them in as I live in a London flat on the third floor, but their story had touched my heart, so it became my quest. On recommendation from a friend who had helped strays, I contacted an animal friendly editor of a national newspaper and asked for his help. He agreed to run a story as long as I would be photographed with the dogs, to which I agreed.

On my way down to Croftview Kennels in Kent, I have to admit that I was very nervous. What if the Kennels were awful and the dogs were not looked after – what would I do?! My fears were allayed as soon as we arrived. I was welcomed by a lovely lady called Kathy Mantripp, who runs this particular branch, and duly met Gracie and Joe and all the other dogs. The kennel was meticulous and the dogs were well looked after. I initially knew little about greyhounds but now know them to be the most gentle, sweet, lovely dogs – they have marvelous natures and make great pets.

Anyway, to cut a long story short, I had my photo taken with these two gorgeous creatures, and a story ran in a Sunday National Paper. After a few unsuccessful enquiries, they finally found a lovely home in the countryside and are now, thankfully, happy and well. I agreed to become a patron of *The Retired Greyhound Trust*, because of the wonderful work they do, continually finding homes for these dogs who are tragically dumped by the racing fraternity when they are too old to race. It really is a terrible state of affairs, and without greyhound rescue charities these beautiful creatures would perish. Enjoy the book and please support greyhound rescue.

Twiggy Lawson

A Greyhound Love Story,

By Judy Jones, America

While on duty as a corrections officer, on the night of September 23rd, 1991, I happened upon a *People* magazine. Inside was an article about a dog track veterinarian who was designated by the dog racing industry to destroy dogs who were no longer winning at the track. The article showed him and his wife surrounded by about six greyhounds. They had eventually begun adopting the dogs out as opposed to destroying them. I was totally shocked and intrigued by the article.

Following two years of various incidents in my personal life, and still having that article on greyhounds on my mind, I started to research the possibility of getting one. At that time, Michigan had only three or four adoption groups, none of which I was impressed with. So, on a trip to my vet one day, I asked him if he had any greyhound clients. He said he had all of one. I requested he put me in touch with her and that led to me contacting the *National Greyhound Adoption Program*, in Philadelphia, Pennsylvania.

After receiving their information, reading up on what to expect with a former racing dog, fencing in my back yard and "getting ready" for my dog, Princess flew into Kalamazoo on July 7th 1993. As she stepped out of the flight crate, she looked up and around, as if to say, "O.K, you may bow and grovel now." Thus, I named her Princess.

A short while after Princess came to live with me, my mother's health deteriorated to the point where it became necessary to admit her to a nursing home facility. This is where Mom met my girl for the first time. The staff were absolutely enchanted with Princess and when we would go to visit they would scurry around and find a blanket for her to lay on, so she wouldn't have to lay on the cold tile floor.

The National Greyhound Adoption Program required a six-month up-date report to see how things were going. My report ended up in

the form of a poem, "Ode to a Greyhound," which to my surprise
was published in their newsletter later in the fall of 1993, following
the passing of my Mom. To everyone's surprise, friends and family
alike, Princess was with me through the visitations and funeral of
my Mom. Being single and not having any siblings, Princess was all
I had. She was a pillar of strength to me through this very sad time
of my life, my father having passed on some years before, leaving me
all alone.....except for Princess.

As the adoption book suggested, I took Princess to obedience school.
I informed the instructor we were not here to sit down and do all the
other "obedience" things, except recall, but were here to complete the
bonding between Princess and myself. The first time I had to turn her
over to one of the instructors, walk to the other side of the schooling
area and call her, my heart was literally in my throat. She took off
so fast that they had to adjust the rubber matting on the floor!

A few weeks after adopting Princess, I happened to watch a National
Geographic segment on television concerning dog racing and what
really happens to the majority of dogs once they are no longer fit for
racing. To sit and watch these beautiful, gentle dogs being disposed of
like garbage sent me off the couch, wrapping my arms around Princess
and crying like a baby. It was shortly after that I got involved with the
Greyhound Protection League.

Back in 1993 greyhound adoption was not as popular or as well
known as it is today, so I decided, because Princess couldn't speak
for herself, I could and I would. I started setting up informational
table events at local pet stores and the annual "Dog Walk"
event sponsored by our local Humane Society. Before I knew it we
were doing as many events as we could to educate the ignorant public
as to why dog racing should be banned or boycotted, and handing out
information on adoption. It was through adopting greyhounds that my
"Greyhound Family" grew and grew.

Due to the incredible history of the greyhound, I investigated various
historical events in and around the Kalamazoo area that I could get

involved in. The first one that I attended was the Silver Leaf Renaissance Faire, an event which celebrates all things Medieval. By this time, I had also adopted a beautiful red brindle boy, named Curly Joe. He was a three time loser, and I was going to "just foster" him until he found a home. Well, he came to my house and never left. So, I was then up to two.

In the early days of Silver Leaf, we made quite an impression as I had hand-out materials on the history of the dogs during the Medieval period, when they were gifts between Kings and Queens. I explained how they had degenerated from that to a disposable commodity of the racing industry. People were appalled.

Silver Leaf led us to the Scottish Festival, which led us to the Irish-American Festival and on and on it went. Of course all my greyhound family helped with these events, and at one point we had close to a dozen hounds and as many adopters in attendance.

One year at Silver Leaf, incredibly enough, they had us set up straight across from the live rabbit exhibit! I thought I had my foot on Princess' leash but apparently not, as all of a sudden this flash of fawn went flying across the pathway and just missed getting this big rabbit that was being picked up off the grass at the time! I apologized to the rabbit people, but of course, one wasn't enough for Princess. I spotted her as she got about half way across the path, yelled at her and she came back to me. Needless to say, everyone who saw that just about fainted away with surprise to see this happen!

Princess and Curly Joe led to the adoption of Missy, so now we had two girls and one boy. I was still working at the Sheriff's Department at the time and nobody could believe I had "gotten another one!" I'm sure they all thought I was crazy.

In November 2004, Princess took a turn for the worse, having been on heart medicine for two years. It was one of the worst days of my life.

Well, over the years Princess, Curly Joe and Missy have all crossed the Rainbow Bridge, but now Jack, Lady, McDu and Velvet call my home their home. Two of them are nine and have been with me for five years. The other two are four. McDu, a big white boy came to me shortly after he turned two. He and I went to dog school and yes, he did learn to sit, to down, but the recall, that's a whole story in itself.

Shortly after Princess went to Heaven, the folks I had adopted several dogs from happened to stop by and we hugged and cried over the loss of Princess, but then the conversation took a turn. They had a load of dogs coming in the following month. I must have had a big "S" for sucker on my forehead as Jo Ann asked what sex and colour I wanted. I asked for a female and said the colour didn't matter. Well, the day the hauler came in, Jo Ann immediately called me and said I wouldn't believe my eyes. Out of one of the holes in the hauler came an almost identical Princess. Without hesitation I told her I'd be up the following week to pick up Velvet. It was difficult, to say the least, to see a reincarnation of Princess before my eyes, but that didn't stop me from bringing her home.

Words cannot express the changes in my life due to the love of one dog. My life went from chaos to a purpose. I went from being a loner to having friends all over the country and the world. I truly believe that Princess had a "paw" in sending Velvet to me so I wouldn't miss her so much. This may sound a little weird, but I don't believe the Lord put the word greyhound in Proverbs 30:29-31, in the Bible for nothing.

Along with all our regular events, we also do pet visitation at some of our local nursing homes and have even done a couple of "Children's Time" at churches, focusing on the story of Noah's Ark being the first animal rescue in history.

My wish is to see an end to dog racing and the greyhound, once again, regaining its status of royalty. One can only dream and hope.......

Along Came Bill,

By Jean Barford, England

It had always been my ambition to own and qualify a show greyhound
and to enter it at Crufts. When I started to exhibit in the small
Exemption Dog Shows about five years ago, I really got the bug.
As time went by I was still getting so much enjoyment out of it, I
started to look for a good line in pedigree greyhounds. I chose the line
I wanted and even put my name down for a puppy when the next
litter was due. In the meantime, I was still enjoying the exemption
shows with Murphy, my rescued veteran ex-racing greyhound

Each time I received my *Greyhound Rescue West of England* magazine,
I tried very hard not to look at the dogs needing a home, because I felt
that two dogs (Murphy and a show greyhound) would be my limit. I
must admit that deep down I had a guilty conscience about waiting for
a show greyhound when so many ex-racing dogs needed a loving home.
Anyway, a sponsorship form for the *Greyhound Rescue West of
England's* walk came through the post and I decided to participate.
When the day arrived my husband, John, Murphy and I set off to the
village of Cradley in Worcestershire.

Now at this point, I must admit that I had some knowledge about a
certain dog, having read about him in *Greyhound Rescue West of
England's* magazine. It said that two greyhounds had been found
wandering the streets, both in very poor condition and been named
Bill and Ben. I also knew that Ben had been lucky enough to be
re-homed, but Bill, who had been in a worse condition, was still in
kennels. I had an urge to look for him. I knew that some of the
greyhounds looking for a home would be brought to the walk and I
needed to get him out of my mind.   .

When I arrived at the walk I asked where Bill was, but no one
seemed to know, so Murphy and I decided to complete our walk and
look for Bill on our return. This done, whilst drinking a well-earned
cup of tea, a gentleman approached me and asked if I was the lady

that was enquiring about Bill. I looked at the dog that stood by his side; a gentle greyhound with sadness in his eyes, who also had many sores, where I am told that his bones had actually broken through his skin. I knelt down and held his gentle head in my hands, and looked into his small sad eyes. I held that memory in my mind and Bill was in my thoughts for days after. He had penetrated my heart.

Then I had an idea; I would offer to foster Bill until he was well enough to be re-homed. After the home check had been completed, Bill came to begin his fostering with us. In the meantime, my husband had been tracing Bill's pedigree by reading his ear markings. He discovered that Bill was an Irish dog, eight years old and his registered name was "Carn Why."

The next few weeks were terrible. Poor Bill lost weight, had diarrhoea, which seemed to go on forever, and his feet became sore. The only good thing so far was that Murphy had accepted him. Bill was on a wheat gluten free diet, but I believe in dogs having proper food such as chicken, beef, fish and rice mixed with a quality mixer biscuit. After about five weeks Bill started to improve and began to show his acceptance of me by giving a slow tail wag and a softening expression in his eyes. He was also taking more interest in things going on around him. He started barking when he was in his run to tell me he wanted to do his toilet duties out in the field rather than in his run. I realised that Bill could soon come into our home because he was becoming house trained.

I felt that Bill had more love for my husband than me at first, because all I ever seemed to do was wash his bottom, push pills down his throat, clean his teeth or pick stones out of his sore feet. He did not understand all this and probably disliked me for it, but it had to be done. I don't know why it all went wrong in the first few weeks. Perhaps I tried too hard to build him up, gave him food that was too rich for him, trying to walk him when his feet were too tender, hoping that by walking him it would give him hope and bring him out of his despair. I was trying too hard, but all is fine now. Bill is very clean, he lives in the house, he has a good diet of fresh food, his walking routine is well under way and he goes swimming once a week with Murphy in our nearby equine and canine swimming pool. Bill now weighs 33 kg. He weighed only 27 kg when he came to us in June 1997.

Since 18th June 1997 Bill has won twenty rosettes (six are first placings), one shield and one cup. I have shown him in Best Rescue and Best Veteran classes. More recently, Bill won a very big event. Out of a class of nineteen other entrants at "The Milton Keynes Festival of the Greyhound" Bill won the "Best Dog for *Retired Greyhound Trust*" Trophy for ex racers, eight years and over. He was presented with a burgundy and gold braid coat, a twelve inch cup and a first place rosette. There was a panel of five judges to judge the class, so having won we stood on the rostrum to have our photo taken.

Can you imagine how very proud of Bill we are? We are so proud of the showing success and could never have wished for more and yet at the same time we have pride in knowing that we were able to re-home him and give him all the love he so much needed. He is living again and gives us more and more love each day. It is a wonderful feeling to know that we have brought a dog back from such despair and sadness. Bill may not be up to Crufts standard, but I am sure you will agree he is already a winner.

Ami, Bob, and Milly,

By Annie Boddy, England

Over the past fifteen years, before my group, A*ction For Greyhounds U.K,* became the successful campaigning group it is today, I have been involved with the rescue, rehabilitation and re-homing of so many greyhounds.

First there was Milly, a dear little blonde girl, aged five. She had been raced at Yarmouth then moved onto somewhere else, after having a toe amputated, which slowed her down. She was then raced at Peterborough, swapped for a Persian cat, raced at a flapping track, ending up in Norwich where two drug addicts who wanted to sell her for £20 lugged her around the city. They took her to a shop, where the owner felt so sorry for her that she gave them the £20 for cold, timid, hungry, skinny Milly.

I had several rescued lurchers at the time, which someone mistook for greyhounds and told the shop owner about me. Eventually, she asked me to help Milly, I took her in and that was it. Milly spent the rest of her years with us and lead a full happy life with the company of all the other dogs and lots of fun and freedom.

We lost her, at age fifteen and a half to cancer. She was my first greyhound. She never put a foot wrong, and was loved by everyone who met her when she accompanied us on the many stalls we do.

After acquiring Milly, I gradually got to learn a lot about racing greyhounds and I realised just how many were bred, raced and disposed of. I wanted everyone to know what I had learnt and after meeting some likeminded people who became good friends and valued supporters, *Action for Greyhounds U.K* was established in 1999.

Since then we have gone from strength to strength, not only raising awareness but doing fundraising stalls in and around Norfolk, leafleting bookmakers' shops and demonstrating outside greyhound stadiums. We also join up with other *Greyhound Action* groups across the country, attending their demos. Letter writing to M.Ps, governments here and abroad, local councils and newspapers is also a very important part of our campaigning. We have held three very successful and well attended Greyhound Remembrance Days each July since 2003, outside Great Yarmouth Greyhound Stadium.

We have raised the awareness of the public as well as being able to home many unwanted racing greyhounds into loving homes. Although *A.F.G UK* can only take in and arrange foster homes on a small scale, as we do not have any kennels, they come to live with us for a while. As part of the family they become socialised with the other dogs, and sometimes cats, before they go to their permanent homes. We make sure they are all neutered or spayed, which we fund and make sure all inoculations and flea and worm treatments are up to date. We also ensure they are the correct weight and in a fit condition, as well as working out their good and bad points before we find them their permanent home.

Poor little Ami was bred in Ireland and just one of the greyhounds we have helped. She was a black and white female and was twelve when *Action For Greyhounds U.K* took her in. What a state she was in! She was raced until she was about six years old, at what we believe was a flapping track. She had been raced at other stadiums too, but we couldn't find out as much as normal about her, as the records had been destroyed. They only keep them for a few years after they retire from racing.

When she was no longer any good for racing her owner or trainer was going to put her to sleep, but a local elderly lady with an old cat asked to have her. She obviously felt so sorry for her but had little idea of how to look after her. Apparently she was fed on dinner scraps, was always in a poor condition and had no veterinary treatment. After the old lady died a teenage girl persuaded her mother to let her have her. The mother had no interest in Ami and the teenager soon grew tired of her, so she ended up with her grandparents. They were very house proud and didn't want Ami living in their bungalow, so she was kept in the garden shed.

When we picked her up we took our dogs with us. Ami seemed overwhelmed by their company. When we were ready to leave, our dogs jumped into the back of the van, followed eagerly by Ami, who never looked back. It was as if she felt she belonged with our dogs and needless to say, they all accepted the dear, gentle, frail old lady. However, the bewildered look Ami had in her eyes that day always seemed to stay there.

In the days after she arrived, we realised Ami had a serious problem with her mouth. Our vet had never seen a worse case of decaying, rotten, unattended dental disease. The vet would have preferred Ami to have had a bit more weight on her but after a six day course of antibiotics and mouth wash to try and eliminate the infection in her mouth and gums, the vet went ahead and gave her a full dental. She was concerned because of the poor condition of Ami that the infection could have spread to her internal organs. Most of her teeth were so rotten that they came out easily and the remaining few were cleaned as best as they could be. Ami pulled through well and it definitely made a difference. She came on leaps and bounds, aided by four nutritious meals a day. Over the next few months we took this down to three, then two.

For the next two years she looked a very good healthy girl, for thirteen or fourteen years old. She was a big girl, long and tall. Her legs and tail seemed to go on forever! She had a little run every day; we called it her "mad five minutes on the field." Ami enjoyed sunny days and always loved to be lying in the garden in the full sun.

At fourteen and a half she had a stroke. She recovered quite well, but of course went a bit wobbly and slowed down a lot. Over the following few months, she had two more small strokes. At the age of fifteen her liver was suffering through old age and the strokes, no doubt exacerbated by the poor treatment she had received before we had her. It was unfair to let Ami deteriorate any further, so we had to make the decision to let her go with the kindness that the vets can give them and slip away peacefully, with dignity.

All we can say to the people who had her before, was that it was an honour to give Ami three years of love and happiness, freedom and the company of all her doggy friends. It is awful that they could never give her the same. We were so happy to have her in our lives for such a short time.

Another greyhound that shared our home was Bob, a black and white male. At five years old he was considered no longer good enough for racing at Yarmouth so was homed by their Homefinders scheme. His new owners could no longer keep him, as, after eight months, they discovered their youngest child was allergic to him. *Yarmouth Homefinders* said they could not take him back. As it was nearing Christmas, local sanctuaries could not accommodate him either. *So Action For Greyhounds* U.K took him in, hoping we could find the perfect home after Christmas and the New Year.

Sadly, we only had him for twelve weeks. He had several small fits but then they got worse and lasted longer. One Saturday evening he had a small fit, then a longer one, an hour and a half later. We phoned the vet who told us to keep him quiet in a dark room and if he fitted again to cover his eyes with a sheet. Keeping him quiet was hard with our young baby and other dogs.

We were going to put him on epilepsy medication from the vet's first thing Sunday morning. This was not to be as Bob did not come out of the last fit he had at midnight. We had to take him to the vet's at 4a.m the next morning, where they confirmed it was a brain stem condition or brain tumour and so he had to be put to sleep.

He was a wonderful, gentle boy, who could be trusted with anything; babies, children, dogs or cats. He was so loving. We miss him so much.

Bess,

By Judy Zatonski, England

If you are sitting comfortably – then I'll begin my tale
I'm a pretty little black colleen – from the Emerald Isle I hail.
Let me introduce myself I'm Bess - yes that's my name
But I'm not like 'Bessie Bunter' - of literary fame
'Cos she was quite a buxom girl and I am very slight
(I needn't watch my waist and hips as many others might!)
I'm also known as Ballintee Pet - 'cos I used to race it's true
Us greyhounds have 'official' names – and we have 'pet' names too!
As I have said, back in my youth – I really loved to race
How fast I flew around that track and enjoyed the thrill of the chase.
Now time passed by and I slowed down but still I tried my best
When I was bumped and hurt my leg – they thought that I should rest.
My leg was bad, the healing slow, my injury may return
Because I could no longer race – my keep I could not earn.
My racing days now at an end... a home was found for me
This wasn't quite the happy place that it was meant to be!
I thought the people loved their Bess – it seems it wasn't so
Without my knowledge they had planned – this little girl should go...
And so they put me in the car – and drove away from home
They dropped me off and set me loose – and left me all alone.
Thirsty, hungry, tired and cold, I wandered aimlessly
(There surely must be someone - who would love and care for me?)
For days and days I walked the streets – I'd sores and lost my fur.
One day..............a lady pulled up in a van and took me off with her...
We ended up at kennels – oh! how damp and cold were they
And I didn't understand the words – "She's only seven days"
I didn't look a pretty sight – my future seemed quite bleak
With just a single day to go – before I'd 'done' my week.....
Someone said "Shall we try 'SAD' – (That's Auntie Shirley's place)
And when Auntie Shirley saw me – the tears streamed down her face
And so 'twas in the nick of time that Shirley rescued me
She sorted out a foster home where I lived happily.
With daily baths and lots of meals, with love and tender care

This pretty greyhound blossomed – four years I had been there...
When my foster Mum was taken ill – no longer could I stay
And so it was the second time that Shirley 'saved the day'
She found a lovely home for me – with Chris in Worcestershire
Her dogs have made me welcome and I'm really happy here
I live with Sophie, Tony too – with him I have such fun
We 'see off' garden 'visitors' – gosh – you should see them run!
I'm still quite slim but healthy now – I couldn't want for more
In bed I wear a nightshirt – but I'm not a girl to snore!
My Mum is always raising funds - for those less fortunate
So lots of people visit us – we dogs think it's just great
'Cos we get lots of human treats – 'their' biscuits taste so nice
"Bess - would you like this piece of cake?" - I don't need asking twice!
That I was born in '92 – did I forget to say?
But now that I've run out of space – I must be on my way!

Blue Bob's story,

By Fiona E. Reekie, Scotland

We had been taking in rescued and unwanted greyhounds for six years when we decided we would take on another poor wee soul. We had recently moved to a bigger house, with a bigger garden and our current two 'hooligans', Lizzie the greyhound and Colin the lurcher, were really settled so the time felt right. Our first stop was the *Dogs Trust* re-homing centre in West Calder. They didn't have any greyhounds but would let us know if one came in. The very next day they phoned us, saying that there was a greyhound called Blue at the Kenilworth re-homing centre. He was extremely frightened of people and they knew it was unlikely that he would be re-homed because of this. If we were interested they would bring him up to Scotland. We agreed immediately and visited him the day after his arrival. We'd expected to see a very scared soul but Blue was beyond scared. He was so psychologically damaged and had clearly been abused. We tried to take him for a little walk to get to know him, but he wouldn't move at all. He was frozen to the spot and shaking violently. We'd never seen anything like it, and I admit I couldn't stop crying on the journey home. We still went ahead and adopted him, but we knew it was going to take him years to gain some confidence. Luckily he hit it off with our other two straightaway and we hoped that their confidence would eventually rub off on him.

It's been just over two years now and he's going from strength to strength. He's turned into a raving lunatic too! Every morning, he comes down for his breakfast, gets a good bum scratch from me, while staring out of the window, making faces at anyone who passes. When we first got him, he used to run and hide when the leads came out. Now, when he feels like a walk, he stands up and starts 'shouting' at the top of his voice and jumping up and down. His one and only trick is lying on his back and waving to you. He also loves to run at you, skid to a halt and start grinning at you! He's come such a long way but he is still scared of strangers. One day I'm sure he'll realise not everyone is going to beat him.

We now believe that everything was 'meant to be' because of the way he's settled in and the way he's bonded with our other two dogs. But not just that. One day I was browsing the Internet when I came across a database of registered greyhounds. I already had both Lizzie and Blue's racing names and dates of birth, so I entered them to get their family trees. I had printed them off and sat down to look at them. It was then I realised that everything was 'meant to be'. Lizzie and Blue were related, and not that distantly. This felt like quite a remarkable co-incidence. Both dogs came from Ireland. Lizzie was rescued locally and came to live with us. Blue was found abandoned and was taken to the *Dogs Trust* re-homing centre in Kenilworth, and then was brought to West Calder and from there to us in Fife.

For some reason, a week ago, I decided to have another look at Blue's pedigree. Whilst doing this, I entered the details of our old greyhound, Pauline, who died a few years ago. To my utter surprise, I discovered she was quite closely related to Blue and to Lizzie as well! This, of course, reduced me to tears! It was very strange as Pauline had an English tattoo and Lizzie and Blue were Irish, but it was there in black and white! What a special wee family we have!

Bonnie,

By Sue Cole, England

Dear Bonnie came to live with me, in November 1994, when she was about two and a half years old. She had been at the *R.S.P.C.A.* home, in Norwich, for about eighteen months, after being involved in an accident, where she was hit by a car and left on the side of the road. Thankfully, she was taken in by the *R.S.P.C.A.*, who paid for her to have all the treatment necessary and to repair her badly broken leg. Her recovery took about a year as her leg had been pinned.

Towards the end of 1994, Bonnie, or "Ronnie" as she was called then, had become a long stay resident at the *R.S.P.C.A.* home and I heard, from a friend, that no one was prepared to adopt her. So, the next day, I went to the kennels and she was brought out for me to see. The carer was very kind to her and it was obvious that he was attached to her. She was quite tiny and looked a bit frail but she was wagging her tail. As soon as she licked my hand it was clear that little Bonnie would soon be living with me.

Bonnie was a very special dog. She was gentle and kind to all she met. She was quiet but sensitive and although the tiniest of all of my dogs, she knew how to look after herself! Bonnie loved her place on the settee and if any of the other dogs took it, she would do her best to get it back as soon as possible. On one occasion, I noticed her standing on the back door step, barking. I wondered what she was up to because she was not one to bark much at all. However, all became clear as quickly all the other dogs, including the one who had been in her place, dashed outside to see what Bonnie had been barking at. Bonnie immediately ran back into the house and jumped on to the settee! What a clever dog!!

Her nearest claim to fame, that I know of, was when she came 'runner up' in the class for 'Dogs that hadn't won any prizes', at the *R.S.P.C.A.* dog show, in the summer of 1997. Bonnie received a certificate, a blue rosette and a goody bag of doggy treats which she shared with her 'brothers and sisters' on her return home.

I have many happy and funny memories of her. I bought my current home from a friend. Before I lived there I went to visit her and took Bonnie and dear Danny (another of my rescued greyhounds) with me. My friend kindly allowed them to roam free around the house. Suddenly, I became worried when I couldn't see either of the dogs but, thankfully, they were soon found... My friend called me to come and see. There was Bonnie, on their settee, watching Crufts on the television!

Bonnie's intelligence was in evidence the one and only time she managed to escape, just after I had moved to this new area. While I was out frantically searching for her, she had made her way home and stood waiting on the doorstep to be let in.

Bonnie went through a number of trials in her life. The pin in her leg made it difficult for her to do all that she wanted. She loved running around like a mad thing but if she did too much she would suffer in the evenings and appeared to be in some pain. Also, in the last couple of years of her life, she had two operations to remove cancerous lumps. This surgery was successful but left her weaker and then her heart began to give her problems. She spent more and more time on the settee, watching what was happening around her but she still loved to have a ride out in the car and she adored the attention of children, never minding any number of hands stroking her.

I feel very privileged that this gentle, loving little dog lived with me for ten years until her death on Tuesday, 23rd, November 2004. I still miss her, dreadfully, even though over a year and a half has passed since she died. I know that I will miss her, forever. Greyhounds are such special dogs and generally very kind, loving animals. They deserve so much and ask so little in return.

Cassi,

By Louise Round, England

I had only been working at *Dogs Trust* Ilfracombe Rehoming Centre for a few months (and had already taken home a seventeen year old lurcher) when a beautiful brindle greyhound was brought in as a stray. Cassi was born in Ireland and spent some time in a Scottish kennels, before somehow ending up in North Devon. I believe she was a coursing greyhound and her original name was "Sybil Ocean." Apparently, she had been found wandering through a North Devon village and a woman had taken her in, with a view to keeping her, but changed her mind when she discovered she wasn't house-trained.

Anyway, as we already had four dogs at home, I decided that the best option was to find Cassi a loving new home. However, after several weeks of not finding the right family to take her on, a friend finally said to me 'For goodness sake, just take her home and have done with it, as you're never going to find her a home that's good enough!'

So, the next step was to win over my husband, Dave. I'd already taken lots of photographs of Cassi and put them around the house, for example on the fridge and in his wardrobe, so he knew what I wanted! After a week of my constantly dropping her name into every conversation he finally woke up on Saturday morning and told me to get up and get dressed as we were going to get her!

After a quick detour to the local pet shop for a new collar and lead, we arrived at the re-homing centre to pick her up and take her out for a long walk in some nearby woods. I knew that she wasn't cat safe and I was a bit unsure as to what she was like with small dogs. When we came face to face with a couple of Westies and all she did was sniff them to say hello, I assumed she'd be alright.

She settled in really well with our other dogs, although she did prove to be a bit of a ringleader in the chewing stakes. We lost count of how many sofa cushions she destroyed; she seemed to have an irresistible attraction to foam! We never did manage to completely house-train her, but the accidents got less and less as she got older!

I can still remember the first time we let her off the lead, on the burrows, near our local beach, and seeing her on the top of a sand dune about half a mile away. She was panting and wagging her tail like her life depended on it! Half an hour later, when she still wouldn't come back, I started to tire of the game, especially as the only way we could eventually catch her was by jumping off a dune and rugby-tackling her to the ground. Needless to say, she thought this was great fun!

Cassi became best friends with our deerhound, Lily, and also proved herself to be a great mate to my brother's two children. She had the most beautiful eyes, which always shone out of her face, even as she got older and her dark muzzle started to turn grey. She was a friendly, fun-loving, cheeky girl who loved a good cuddle. I always thought I was special to her, as the first time I met her she leaned on me for a hug and rubbed her head against my legs. However, it soon became apparent it was nothing personal. I would often find her snuggling up to someone else on the beach when I let her off the lead.

She had a huge capacity for life, so it was with great sadness that we discovered last year that she had cancer of the jaw. It was a huge decision to decide whether or not to let her have an operation to remove the tumour, but after talking to our lovely vet and the specialists in Bristol, we decided it was worth it to improve her quality of life and give her extra time. To our delight, she sailed through the operation; the only after-effect being that her tongue often lolled out of one side of her mouth as she didn't have enough teeth to stop it! She actually lived another pain-free, happy eighteen months, but the cancer sadly returned elsewhere in her body and we had to make the awful decision to put her to sleep. Fortunately, the end came very quickly and one of my last memories is of her running through nearby fields with a big grin on her face...

Connor,

By Lisbeth Larsen, Denmark

This story begins with the death of my nine-month old whippet. His name was Alex and even though more than a year has passed since he crossed the rainbow bridge, I still miss him very much. The best way to honour his memory is to go on living and loving, and this led to a new beginning with a new dog, although no one can replace Alex.

My other whippet, Mike, and I missed having another dog, so I started to look for a new family member. One of my friends knew of my love for greyhounds so he surfed the net and found an organisation called *Galgos in Need, Denmark*. I had no idea what a galgo was, so I called the Chairman and we talked about sighthounds for well over two hours. As a result, I asked her to find me a galgo. Ten days later she called me to tell me that she had one and would I be interested in him. Needless to say I was intrigued and said, "Yes." She told me that he was a large brindle dog with a very gentle character. His name was Cadete. She then sent some pictures and I fell in love with him. He was to arrive on the 22nd of March 2005. Late at night on the 21st, she called me to say that he was too traumatised to make a good pet, but she had found another brindle dog with the sweetest character. She asked if I would consider him instead of Cadete. I said, "Yes" so it was agreed that she would bring him home to me.

The next day I went to the airport to pick up my new family member. There, I met the second in command of the charity and signed the adoption papers. She showed me a picture of my new dog, and to my surprise he was a pure bred greyhound and not a galgo. I was delighted, as I love greyhounds. Finally, two dogs came out of customs and my greyhound's crate was unloaded. Out tumbled this drop dead gorgeous young greyhound. It was love at first sight.

Now that a year has almost past, I can honestly say that I have no regrets. Before he came to me he had an awful life. Connor was found starving to death in front of the main gate of the royal palace in Madrid, at the tender age of thirteen months. Someone called Pedro took pity on him and tried to give him a little milk but Connor would not or could not drink it. Pedro, the palace worker, then called *Galgo Sin Fronteras* and told them about Connor. Christina Garcia came and picked the young greyhound up and nursed him back to health. Had it not been for these kind-hearted people, my beloved greyhound would not be alive today. I gave him the name Connor as Pedro does not suit a regal greyhound such as mine.

I have found tattoos in both Connor's ears, but someone has tried to erase these first tattoos with acid. They have then tattooed poor Connor's ears, three to four times, on top of the original tattoos, so finding Connor's pedigree has turned out to be extremely difficult. However, I have good people to help me, so maybe the true story of how my young greyhound ended up in that predicament will one day come to light. Connor is a greyhound of coursing stock, of that there is absolutely no doubt, so maybe this will narrow our search perimeter.

Mike and I both love Connor, the smiling greyhound, very much, and because of what he has been through I am now deeply involved in trying to save as many greyhounds and galgos as I possibly can. Greyhounds change one's life forever, for the better. Connor has changed ours and I am quite sure that little Alex, my whippet approves.

Duke,

By Maria Park, Scotland

I got a phone call from a friend telling me a fence had blown down in a garden near her house and she could see some greyhounds that were in a bad way. So I went straight there and saw one big black dog that was standing in two inches of muck. He couldn't stand anywhere in his small run without standing in his own waste. His shed didn't have a door on it so I could see inside. There was at least two feet of dirt on the floor.

I went to the house to speak to the owner, who was the dirtiest man I have ever seen. After some hard work I got him to give me all but one of his dogs. I took a brindle bitch who was pregnant, the big black boy, a black and white dog called Duke and a brindle dog called Barnie.

I kept the boy, Duke, myself. I already had three greyhounds so I was more than happy to have him. All the other dogs got good homes and the bitch had seven pups, who all got homes with no problems, with the help of the *Greyhound Awareness League* and the *S.S.P.C.A.*

Duke was in a terrible state. He had about sixty percent of the hair that he should have and was very thin. His coat stank and to touch his ears was very painful for him, due to ear mite infestation, which my vet thought he had had for over a year. The smell from his ears made me nauseous. His skin was very red, as the man had been putting some crazy concoction of cream on him. The greyhound people seem to have a world of their own when it comes to medicine. Old wives' tales seem to have a lot to answer for.

Duke turned out to be the nicest, biggest dog I've ever met. He had the sweetest temperament and never so much as growled at my other three dogs in the five years that I had him. My kids could take him for walks and brush him all over for hours and he just loved every second. We took him to the Sunday market every week and he would walk about with no lead and everybody knew him and thought he was brilliant. One day at the market, a man, who said Duke was called "Emulsion" and that he had bred him, approached me. I told him where and how I had got him and it turned out he had raced him for some years and done very well with him. Then the guy I got him from had brought him. When I showed the man the photographs of Duke when I got him he was really angry.

I always thought I would have Duke for a very long time but unfortunately he got bone cancer in his leg. It all started with him limping for no apparent reason, so we took him to the vet, who I know well. I mentioned that I knew these dogs were prone to bone cancer. She nodded. I had to phone later that day. When I spoke to the vet she said, "You were right." I knew what she meant and, for once, I wish I had been wrong.

There was no treatment. I could keep him alive on painkillers but I couldn't do that to him. So, we decided I would give it a week to make my mind up. I made sure he had a great time; treats, bones, walks and cuddles.

His limp was getting worse and he would scream sometimes, even with the painkillers. I was being selfish so I phoned the vet and made an appointment. I drove to the vet's in tears; I could hardly see the road. I decided to take him for one last walk on the way. He ran around like a young pup. I could hardly believe I was about to put him to sleep. I couldn't. I phoned the vet to cancel my appointment but, just as I got my phone out of my pocket, he came to an abrupt halt and gave the worst scream ever. I knew I had to take him. The phone went back in my pocket. I'm sure you know the rest. I am just glad I was able to make some of his years great fun.

Frankie,

By Nancy Rohde, America

Frankie joined our family about eight years ago. He was a big, handsome, brindle boy and from the first moment we saw him we knew he was truly a gentle, happy soul! He was also very intuitive. The day we went to pick him up, he just knew he was coming with us and that we were his new Mom and Dad. We witnessed this in his actions as he went in search of a chewy bone from the rescue kennel, to take with him to his new home with us.

Through the years he brought us so much love and sweetness. He loved to just gaze at us from across the room with those wonderful doe eyes. He was very sensitive and responded to our kindness and affection as well. He even learned to like our cat, Sadie. He was very polite and respectful of her.

Frankie was our first greyhound, so we were pretty inexperienced at transitioning him into our lives, but he showed us the way. His eyes and facial expressions always told us how he felt and he would smile and shiver all over to greet us. We would tuck him in every night on his big soft bed with his favourite blanket and he would groan in appreciation every time!

He loved to cuddle and be with us where ever we were. He adored playing with his favourite rubber ball. When he would lose it under a piece of furniture, he would always show us where it was by pointing and staring at the spot where it went under. We would say, "Where's your ball?" and he would run to the spot.

He was always a perfect gentlemen and when we adopted another dog, Ginger, he let her become the boss. He watched out for her and she for him. They were always together. Frankie and Ginger's personalities were both unique, but they had the same basic greyhound gentleness and sweetness about them!

At twelve years old, he has gone onto doggie heaven just this past August, but he is still here with us every day, warming our hearts. Frankie brought such joy to our lives, and we will forever feel his sweet presence.

Gem and Alfie,

By Annie Boddy, England

Gem is a black and white female. She was only five years old when *Action for Greyhounds U.K* took her in. She has to be the worst greyhound cruelty case we have had to deal with so far.

She was bred in Ireland, raced in Kent, then sent to a trainer in Yarmouth. Next, she was advertised free in the local *Ad Trader* paper, by someone who helps trainers give away their greyhounds quickly. A few months after acquiring Gem, her new owners advertised her in the same paper, free with no home-check, and still not spayed or inoculated. The ad said that she didn't get on with their cats. She went to a flat in a Norwich where there were eleven cats. She was terrified of them. In the eight months that this owner had Gem, she literally deprived her of food. We learnt about Gem by chance, just in time to save her.

We will never forget the day we picked her up from the flat. She was covered in fleas and flea dirt, had infected pressure sores, a piece of tail missing and the wound was infected and weeping puss. She weighed only two stone and ten pounds. We were amazed she could still stand and walk. I dread to think where she had been kept. We are glad we didn't stay and look; we just wanted to get her out of there.

We were in shock for the rest of the day but had to get on and bath her to get rid of the fleas, dirt and smell. We cleaned her wounds and sores and took pictures and videos of her to use as evidence if we tried to get the previous owners prosecuted. We fed her small amounts every two hours and she was ravenous. She had a giant beanbag, with a quilt on top, to lay on to make her bony body more comfortable. The next day we took her to the vet's, who immediately called in an *R.S.P.C.A* inspector, who came and took photographs and a statement. The inspector successfully took the case to court five months later. Gem's story got into the local papers and the owner got a five year ban from owning dogs and a £100 fine. She should have got a lifetime ban and they should have taken all her cats away.

We found the original adverts in the *Ad Trader* paper and informed the previous owners of Gem's tragic story, as we feel that they were all responsible for what happened to Gem; the breeders, the trainers, and the owners.

As Gem's short life had been filled with so much misery already and we were the eighth people to have her, we decided to keep her, rather than re-home her again. We knew she would be safe with us. We built her up mentally and physically over the next few months into a happy, healthy young greyhound, who weighed five stone. Then in November, 2004, while we were out walking, she had a horrific accident. Some children had been using a large sheet of corrugated iron as a sledge and left it lying around. We heard a horrific scream. Gem had skinned her leg, from thigh to toe, on the edge of it. I rushed her to the vet's but the leg could not be saved and had to be amputated. Although the operation was very successful, worse was to come. The next morning it was discovered that Gem was a haemophiliac, so her blood wouldn't clot. She had lost lots overnight. It was touch and go, as her red blood cell count was dangerously low. Our other greyhound, Zonda, donated a pint of blood for a transfusion for Gem. Luckily this worked and after six days we had Gem home. She was a skinny girl again, but with such a strong spirit and a great will to live.

It is over a year now and Gem is as fit as before. She can run just as fast now but tires much quicker. However, she takes everything in her stride. She is such a wonderful girl. We hope she never has to suffer any more misfortune. In her short life she has survived so much.

Another dog we rescued, called Alfie, has been through a lot too. We first met him when he was a puppy. A local trainer had bred him. Alfie was taken to our vet's with a broken back leg. The breeder said he had accidentally shut the pup's leg in a door. He paid for the x-ray. However, when he realised the operation would cost about £500 and the pup would need a stabiliser bolt fitted to his leg for several weeks, which would need to be adjusted weekly, he refused to help.

Our vet contacted us to see if we could come to Alfie's aid. It was agreed that the trainer should sign over the pup to our vet, who would then do the operation, which we, *Action for Greyhounds U.K*, would pay for. The pup would then be signed over to us. We, fortunately, had help from donations from three other organisations.

We took the pup home, where he convalesced with his grown up doggy sisters and us for the next few months. He was such a delight and a little scamp too! What an experience it was to help rear a little greyhound pup and know he was never going to see a greyhound stadium or be affected by the awful greyhound racing industry.

Because of Alfie's age and the constant attention he needed, he accompanied us everywhere, including our fundraising events. He was the centre of attention as so many people had never seen a greyhound pup. How many people, apart from the ones involved in the racing industry, are ever likely to see a greyhound puppy? What is even more frightening is where do they all go?

Well, Alfie certainly landed on his feet. After making a hundred percent recovery, at ten weeks old, he went to a country home with a big garden, fields and woods to run in with another ex-racing greyhound for a friend. What could have been better for him?

Alfie was one lucky puppy who survived the racing industry, out of thousands who don't. Ironically our vet says if the trainer/owner had spent the time and money, he would have had a top class racing dog. How lucky we were to be in the right place, at the right time, for Alfie.

He Waited For Me,

By Barbara Masi, America

He left the track in search of a home
And he was again crated and lonely
He promised everyone he wouldn't roam
And he waited for me.

He saw others come and others go
And it seemed to be "homey"
But it wasn't where he wanted to stay
He just waited for me.

He promised to be good and kind
He tried and did succeed
He was always sweet and tried to mind
As he waited for me.

I didn't know he was waiting so long
Two years and a half of his life
If I only knew that he was so strong
As he waited for me.

We found each other – oh, joy – oh, bliss
This brindle boy of glee
He was mine and I was his
No more waiting for me.

I cry as I tell him I didn't know
The things that he did see
I would have been an earlier show
If I knew he was waiting for me.

This is dedicated to Foggy (now Flash)
He waited a very long time at the Greyhound Pets of
America kennel to find his forever home
He was adopted on June 4, 2002,
when he joined the Masi Pack

Isabella, My First Greyhound,

By Jennifer Storm, America

When my corgi passed away I decided I wanted another dog. I sat at my computer to do some research and just by chance I clicked on "greyhounds." That was three years ago.

Online information led me to the *National Greyhound Adoption Program* run by Mr David Wolf, here in the Philadelphia area where I live. I volunteered to walk their dogs and fell in love with one of them, a brindle girl. The kennel had given her the name of Soraya. I loved walking her as she was so gentle and would lean up against me and say "Take me home with you..." She was a galgo, a Spanish greyhound, flown to the United States by a caring Spanish pilot. She had been found in Spain dehydrated, covered in ticks, with a broken leg and left for dead.

I filled out an application to adopt her but then had to leave the country to attend to a sick parent. When I returned, I hurried to the kennel only to find her crate empty! Someone else had adopted Soraya. I simply couldn't believe it!

I struggled to forget her. I walked out other dogs to find one that I felt the same way about but simply couldn't decide. The weeks went by, and then the months. I thought about Soraya so often and she stayed vividly alive in my memory.

Four months later, on April 9th, the phone rang. It was a friend who works at the kennel. She told me that a greyhound had been found roaming the area north of Philadelphia and that a kennel employee had been out in the van to find it. When they brought the dog back, she realized it was Soraya. The owners did not even call to see if their dog had been found. My friend couldn't wait to call me. Early next morning I was at the kennel, overwhelmed with joy. Soraya came home with me; "my heart dog," as greyhound people call their first and most special greyhound. She is the best and most beautiful greyhound, who has an amazing story with a happy ending.

She is now on her way to becoming a Therapy Dog, which means we go and visit old folks homes and bring cheer to the elderly. They love to stroke her and look into her beautiful brown eyes. I changed her name to "Isabella", after one of the Spanish queens and I wrote a poem about her:

Found roaming in the streets alone,
My Isabella, my gentle friend.
Your owner had a heart of stone;
That's how you came to be my own.

The loyalty, the love, the trust
Amaze me time and time again;
That you still find it in your heart
When all you ever knew was pain.

Betrayals are all over now,
You're safe and sound forever.
A life of play and meals and rest,
Is yours, dear Isabella.

Isabella has been with me for almost three years now. She is a different dog to when she first came home with me. She is relaxed, happy and trusting. She owns every couch in our home and just loves living in the lap of luxury. I could never have asked for a more wonderful dog and I cherish every moment I spend with her.

Jagger,

By Ted Wolfenden, England

Jagger, whose racing name was "Manor Lamp", was born in September 1993. He was raced, until November 1998, at Wembley. When Wembley closed down Jagger was transferred to Brighton but it was decided that at five and a quarter years he was too old for racing at that Stadium. He appears to have been taken home either by his trainer or owner and then to have been used for coursing and possibly for breeding.

In January 2001, he was involved in a road accident in the Basing-stoke area. He was taken to a vets, where the Senior Dog Warden got involved. Jagger was then transferred for safe keeping to *Binfield Dog Rescue* in Wokingham, Berkshire.

In February 2001, we had decided to take Jason, our five year old grandson, to the local Shire Horse Centre. However, on arrival, we found this was closed. So we decided we would call at the dog rescue centre and see if there was a dog we could walk with him.

The rescue allowed us to walk a greyhound called Jason. So both Jasons walked each other on the lead! We were very impressed with the way this greyhound walked at the pace of our grandson. Plus, as we walked by one house, there were two guard dogs who started to growl and bark at us. The greyhound moved to position himself between them and our grandson. At that point, my wife said we should offer to re-home this greyhound. It took over a week, as the rescue or dog wardens had been contacted by the greyhound's owners, who had been informed that there were around £150 of charges. The owners then refused to be contacted at all. In the meantime, I was going up everyday to walk the greyhound. On the Friday we were informed that we could foster the greyhound for three months, keeping a record of all costs. After these three months we finally became the official carers of the greyhound now called Jagger.

During those three months we managed to cure Jagger's love of chasing cats; necessary as we had two of our own. We also found out that he had been mistreated, by being hit with a stick. He was afraid of a walking stick or of anyone shouting at him, so much so that he would curl up in a ball and cover his head with his legs to protect himself. We eventually overcame this fear by kindness.

We have never been able to find much of his recorded racing history, except someone else looking for their rescued greyhound's history came across Jagger's name as the winner in all the races both he, and their greyhound, had raced. We also know from his running ability at our local park, where everyone stops to watch Jagger, that he is sheer poetry in motion when running. Whilst racing with another greyhound, Jagger would suddenly turn one hundred and eighty degrees either by a left or right turn, which is why we believe he had been used for coursing.

He has cost our insurance lots of money since we had him. The first incident was due to an attack by a German Shepherd Dog in 2002. It took six hours of surgery to save his life. In 2003, whilst running at the park, on attempting a turn, his back leg went into a rabbit hole, resulting in him sliding across the park on his left side for about thirty metres and getting a broken left hock. In October 2004, a calcified spinal disc, in his neck, exploded. This resulted in him having two major spinal operations. He came home with us on November 17th, 2004, with less than a five percent chance of ever walking again and a recommendation, by all the professionals, to be put to sleep.

Instead, I contacted Angela at Greyfriars Hydrotherapy Centre, where there is a Physiotherapist on site once a week. Angela stated they would not guarantee Jagger would improve but would do all they could for him. His treatment involved four, fifty-four mile return journeys a week.

We took it in turns to sleep downstairs with Jagger, as he needed to be moved onto a different side every two hours. It also took both of us to carry him outside to carry out his business. On December 27, 2005,

with our help, he walked on all four legs, then on December 31,
he barked and we met him at the door standing on all four legs.
From that day he was changing sides himself and he objected to us
trying to move him.

Jagger is now eighty-five percent fit and takes me and our other dog,
a german shepherd (one of his girl friends, to whom we gave a home
in February 2005 as her owners were off to the U.S.A. and about to
put her to sleep), for an hour walk each morning and up to four
ten minute walks each day. He sleeps all night from eleven p.m.
until eight a.m., downstairs with our german shepherd.

Jed's Story,

By John Ratcliffe, England

Jed was the latest addition to our family of greyhounds. He made
the number up to seven again, after the loss of our lovely Oscar on
25th February, 2002. We also had a small Jack Russell type mongrel,
so that made a nice family of eight dogs.

Jed had been a winner in his early life. We knew that because when
his "owner" asked us to come and collect Jed and take him into our
animal sanctuary, he gave us Jed's racing and I.D. card. From this
we could see that he had been born in Ireland, on 19th July, 1990.
He raced in Cork and Dungannon and soon he had a series of wins,
both at trials and actual races. As time passed he started to come in
fourth and then sixth. Obviously that wasn't what he had been bred
for and somehow Jed found himself in a small town in the north of
England. We don't know what happened after that because there are
no entries on his card for tracks in England. I suspect that he must
have been raced on flapping tracks. These are not controlled by the
National Greyhound Racing Club and conditions for the dogs can be
very poor. If Jed was used on one of these tracks there would be no
entries on his card, which there aren't.

The first time I met Jed was in 1995, when his owner in England rang
the animal sanctuary where my wife and I are trustees and asked if
we could take in a fawn male greyhound. I went to pick Jed up and
he gave me a big grin, for which he soon earned his nickname of the
"laughing greyhound." Whenever someone went up to his pen he used
to curl his lip and simply smile at them, rubbing the side of his head
on the wires so that they could tickle his chin. On reflection, I wish so
much that we had taken him home right then instead of taking him
into the sanctuary, but at that time we had eleven dogs here at home
with us; ten greys and lurchers and the small mongrel. I just wish we
had made room for Jed as well.

I can't recall exact dates but after staying at the sanctuary for probably about a year, someone wanted to take Jed home. We do home-checks before a dog is allowed to be adopted and everything seemed fine at Jed's potential new home so off he went. The staff and trustees were very pleased because they all knew and loved Jed and were happy because he had at last got the home that he deserved.

One day, about two years later, I was at the sanctuary and I saw a greyhound that looked just like Jed. As soon as I approached his kennel he started to smile. I couldn't believe it; Jed was back! I made enquiries but I am sorry to say that I can't remember anything about why he had been returned. To be truthful, I wasn't really interested. Whatever the reason was, it wasn't worth listening to. I vaguely recollect that it was something about him weeing in the house. I do remember that I was totally and utterly disgusted and I began to have serious doubts about the validity of our home-checking policy. Time passed. Every day people came looking for a pet dog but no one wanted Jed. He came out of his kennel and smiled at them, rubbing his face on the wires of his prison. They walked right past him. Further down the row there was a prettier dog; they would probably adopt that one. However, one day a man came and saw Jed. He knew instantly that Jed was the dog for him. The sanctuary arranged a home-check and this time Marilyn and I did it ourselves. He was perfect for Jed. He had an enclosed garden where Jed could run around and he seemed to really want to take him home as soon as possible. Jed went to his perfect home and we were all so happy for him.

In 2001, Jed was back. They were moving to a smaller house. There was no room for him, they said, and anyway, he had started weeing in the house. This time he was clearly unhappy; he began to lose weight and became very lethargic. The vet did some tests but couldn't find anything clinically wrong. They moved him into the "old woofs" building, as Jed was eleven years old now so he qualified for admittance. This is a building where the older dogs go and where they get an extra treat now and then. With all the attention he seemed to improve and regain weight but he was clearly unhappy. Marilyn and I had just lost our Oscar and we realised at long last that Jed belonged with us. We took him home on 31st March, 2002. He fitted in right away. There were no problems accepting all our other dogs, even the Jack Russell, and everything was set for Jed to live happily ever after.

However, on 9th August, 2002, Jed was clearly unwell. His urine was almost purely blood and he was very lethargic. The vet thought it might be an infection and gave him antibiotics and anti-inflammatory drugs. On 12th August, our beloved Jed died. He had been at the vet's surgery since the morning, for blood tests and x-rays. At about 1p.m. the vet rang us, saying he had discovered lots of small tumours on Jed's liver. After a long discussion with the vet we knew we had to let Jed go whilst he was under the anaesthetic. If he woke up he would only have about a week to live and his quality of life would be non-existent.

There have been lots of mistakes along the way in Jed's life. I feel that he has been let down by us. Marilyn and I have vast experience in this field but this last guy fooled even us. By the way, in the five months that we were privileged to have Jed, he never once urinated in the house, not even at the end when he was very sick.

Jess,

By Ruth Boswell, England

Sally Willbie from *Greyhound Rescue West of England* wrote this about Jess:
"In March 2003 after deciding that she and her husband could manage a third greyhound (a new friend for Tara and Holly), Ruth went to the *R.S.P.C.A.* in Birmingham to see a black greyhound, named Shrew. She had been in hospital for eight weeks as she had been run over and then brought in as a stray.

Ruth loved Shrew at first sight but in the next cage was a very sad old greyhound called Jessie. She was on a '7 dayer', due to be put to sleep in two days. She'd been wandering around factory units in Bordesley, was extremely thin and could hardly stand. Ruth decided that she could not be left, especially as she was told that she would only last a few weeks anyway. It was only when standing beside her Peugeot 206 with two extra dogs that Ruth wondered how four dogs would ever fit in! They did though, like jigsaw pieces.

Jessie went from strength to strength. Her rotten teeth were removed, leaving just four canines and she put on two stone. She was a grand old girl with a lovely character. At fourteen years old she was third in the "Big Veteran Class" at the *G.R.W.E.* show."

She had several nicknames, including "Fangs". She was mainly nicknamed "Jessie Jumble" as, although hardly able to stand when we first had her, when passing by a church hall, she ran into the hall where they were holding a jumble sale and made all the ladies scream!

She had a stroke at the age of fourteen and a half and was put to sleep on 20th October, 2004.

Another friend wrote a tribute to her, just after we lost her and I feel the wording really sums up just how she was:

"Jessie Jumble was the most knackered, worn out, bossy, toothless, super special, wonderful greyhound grandma bag of bones that was rescued hours before the *R.S.P.C.A.* were about to put her to sleep. They thought she would only live a week as she was so thin she was painful to look at. Most of her teeth had to be removed and she could barely walk at first because her back legs were all but crippled. However, she still managed to wag her tail and give you a kiss. With Boswell TLC she rolled back the canine clock and had the most fantastic two years of her life. Heartbreakingly, she died a few weeks ago. It was her time but that doesn't stop us all missing her".

I now have five greyhounds. We had our first greyhound from the dogs' home in January 2001. Having never owned a dog before and not being brought up with them, I was apprehensive when my husband said he would like a canine companion. We trawled the various rescue centres for many months and came across our beautiful fawn greyhound. We called her Tara. Within six months, I was the one pestering for another! We adopted Holly through *Hall Green Retired Greyhound Trust*, as by now we had come to hear about the plight of greyhounds. I then got a job managing a vet clinic and by 2003 I had taken on Shrew and Jess. Following a re-mortgage to buy a bigger car and a caravan so we could go on holiday, a few months later, a lovely white greyhound was brought into the vet's to be put to sleep. He was three and a half years old and had finished racing. I took him on hoping to find him a home. He found one with us so we were up to five grey-hounds!!!

Unfortunately, we lost Holly aged seven, with bone cancer and Jess last October at the grand old age of fourteen. Going down to three in the house suddenly felt so quiet so we took on Basil, aged three, through *Perry Barr Retired Greyhound Trust*. Annie also came to live with us at the end of August this year. She is a fourteen year old stray in a poor condition, who came through Greyhound Gap. I love my family of four legged, long nosed 'babies' and could not imagine life without them.

My life has changed beyond belief as I am now a very active member of the *Perry Barr and Hall Green RGT*. I have set up sponsor schemes and 50-50 clubs, write a monthly newsletter, do awareness road shows and help at the kennels in every spare moment, in-between working full time. I help *Greyhound Rescue West of England* where I can and raise money for *Greyhounds in Need* and *GALA*.

Jet's Story,

By Heather Finch, England

She jumped down from the Land Rover and screamed. The kind of scream only a greyhound can make. The kind of scream that stops people in their tracks and forms icicles around their hearts.

She was very small, very thin and shivering. It was a freezing morning and she had no protection from the cold; no body fat, no kennel coat and very little of her own coat.

She held her back leg off the ground and whimpered. 'It's just a tendon injury. Be fine with a bit of rest'. They handed me her lead, a battered, black leather lead and she meekly hobbled to stand near me. I bent to stroke her head and she flinched when the end of the lead came near her.

'Always scared, that one. Sneaky too. Couldn't stand her in the house, so sneaky'.

I was given a small washing up bowl to feed her in, a handful of treats and a muzzle. 'Oh, can we have the muzzle back when you've bought a new one?' They jumped into their Land Rover and were gone.

We stood watching them go, me and the scared, thin, shivering greyhound called Jet.

Over the coming weeks, we learnt more about the little, skinny, black greyhound called Jet. Her racing name had been "Oakfield Cracker" and she'd been born in March 1999. She'd run twenty-four races at the Reading track between January and July 2002. And then her 'official' racing history stopped. She'd been sold on and raced on 'flapper' tracks. That is, until she broke her leg. And of course, her owners carefully tended to that broken leg with veterinary help. Didn't they? *Didn't they?*

No. They left her to scream in agony every time she used that leg. And six months later, they gave her away, with a small washing up bowl to feed her in, a handful of treats and a muzzle.

Now, three years later, she is a healthy, shiny, loving greyhound. She follows me around like a shiny black shadow and is fiercely protective of me. She is still scared of rolled-up newspapers and sudden movements, either by hand or foot. No guessing why that is!

She has broken and worn teeth from when she tried to escape from her cage in the kennels. She's a greyhound terrorist when it comes to other dogs, although she has learnt to live with other greyhounds, with just the odd snarl and snap to put them in their place. And she is sneaky. It's part of her charm. She's bright and intelligent and has learned to look after her own interests, because in the past there was nobody else to rely on.

And her broken leg? You'd never know, unless you looked closely at the deformed bone and the twisted paw.

Judy,

By Mike Kelly, Ireland

I found my small blue greyhound bitch, Judy, wandering the streets about seven years ago. She was crossing the main, dangerous, Bristol Road, in Northfield, Birmingham, and looked starving and distressed. I almost ran her over.

She had just a backbone visible and it took three worming doses, over a month, to resolve all her eating problems. She could not eat solids for weeks and had to have baby foods. My vet said it was the worst case he had seen in thirty years. For weeks she could not walk past bin liners in the street, as this was presumably her only source of food.

She is fifteen now and still loves her walk with Bruno, her inseparable Collie friend. They lie on top of each other in the car and in the house. Judy is now de-stressed and lies in a ball on the chair, her chair. If you sit on it she reclaims ownership by sitting on you.

Cruelty to these dogs by sub-humans just beggars belief.

Kiana and Shannon,

By Kim White, America.

As most true dog lovers will tell you, their dog or dogs are the most unique and special in all the world. I count myself to be among this fortunate group of people as I have the privilege of sharing my life and home with two remarkable dogs. Kiana is a yellow lab and Shannon, her "sister," is a brindle greyhound. I would like to share an amazing, true story that took place last fall.

Kiana, then nine years old, and Shannon, ten, were anxious to get outside and enjoy the nice fall weather. Unfortunately they had been "banned" from going out into the fenced-in yard, as we had recently had some major yard work done. This extensive work was the result of having two, one hundred and thirty foot oak trees fall in the yard. We were told by the landscapers to keep the dogs off the backyard for several weeks, until the new grass was established. Our neighbor, Linda, felt sorry for the girls and told us to bring them over to her yard, to let them romp around a bit. Now, Linda's husband, Elliot, maintains a compost pile in his yard. Kiana and Shannon enjoy fresh veggies when we prepare dinner and they saw this compost pile as a large version of a salad. We were not aware that they had gotten into it. Well, that night was horrible beyond words.

About 1:00am, both Kiana and Shannon began vomiting and having diarrhoea all over the house. We were up with them and could not figure out what was going on. By the morning, Shannon had stopped but Kiana was clearly getting worse. We rushed them both over to our vet's office at 7:30 that Thursday morning. Our vet had us leave Kiana there, but checked Shannon out and gave us clearance to take her home but to carefully monitor her.

Through process of elimination, we determined that while eating from the compost pile they had also ingested fertiliser. Kiana had obviously gotten more of this into her system as her symptoms continued and grew worse. Our vet described it as having her insides burned from the chemicals.

By Friday, Kiana was somewhat stable but very lethargic. She was receiving IV fluids and antibiotics yet showed no interest in any food. We asked if we could visit and bring her sister along as well. So, we loaded Shannon into the car and went to cheer up Kiana. Seeing her lieing in the large cage with these IV's hooked up to her was more than I could take. Her look of pain and near despair brought tears to my eyes. I began to realize how sick she really was and that there was a chance that she might not make it.

Well, I sat on the floor so that I could pet her and look into her eyes, all the while holding Shannon's leash. Before I knew what was happening, Shannon jumped right up into the cage with Kiana, turned around, laid down and put her paws across Kiana's front legs. The vet was astonished, ran to his office and came quickly back to capture this moment on film.

Needless to say, these pictures continue to touch my heart and soul whenever I look at them and share them with others. Kiana's recovery was slow but steady and it is hard to believe that it was a year ago this month when this happened. We came so close to losing her and I believe beyond a shadow of a doubt that Shannon's presence that day inside Kiana's hospital quarters had a profound affect upon her healing. This rang even more true when our vet described to us a few weeks later just how tenuous her condition was during that critical time.

Kiana and Shannon are both a year older now and continue to be very bonded, not only to us but to each other. We feel so blessed to be a part of their lives and to have witnessed this profound moment that they shared last fall.

Lloyd – A Beloved Friend,

By Angela Hogan, England

It was Wednesday, 2nd June, 2004, and we were eagerly awaiting the arrival of another "Golden Oldie" at *Tailends*, our home for elderly dogs. Bobby arrived around lunchtime after his long journey from Kent. *The Retired Greyhound Trust* had again enlisted the help of Nigel Woods to move this old chap from his kennel to a proper home at last. It was while we were chatting to Nigel that he mentioned another old dog, called Lloyd, who was still at the kennel that Bobby had come from, but was not owned by the *Retired Greyhound Trust* but by Ladbrokes, the well-known bookmaker. Nigel said it was such a shame he could not have the chance of a home too, as he was very old and not very well.

When Nigel had set off on the long journey back to St Albans and we had made Bobby comfortable, I decided to make a few phone calls and seek advice on getting Lloyd out of his kennel and into our care. We were desperate for him to receive veterinary attention as soon as possible. We knew he was quite ill and maybe would not have long to live. It was essential that he did not die friendless and maybe in pain, surrounded by the bleak walls of a kennel. Mandy Hooker (who runs *Northants Greyhound Rescue*) wasted no time in arranging with the *Retired Greyhound Trust* office for Lloyd to be released by Ladbrokes into my care.

It was a very hot day on 15th June, 2004, the day Nigel was to bring Lloyd down to Devon. We spent anxious hours waiting and hoping that Lloyd would cope with the journey. He finally arrived at around 5pm and we were so relieved to see him. He was a large frail brown and white boy, with a wonderful face and two huge, sightless, cloudy eyes. The poor chap probably wondered what was happening to him. He had never known anything but life in a kennel for the whole of his thirteen years. His poor mouth was green, foul smelling and full of infection and rotten teeth. He was painfully thin with his ribs protruding out from his chest. He was passing a black tarry liquid stool and we were very glad that we had booked him into the vet the following morning. He did not want any food even though we tried to tempt him. This did not surprise us, considering what he had been through and the state of his mouth.

The next day Lloyd was given a thorough examination by the vet and blood tests were done. It was decided that his mouth was so bad that he needed immediate dental treatment. Infection from his mouth could well be travelling to other parts of his body and causing all sorts of problems. He had to have all his teeth out and was then put on a drip overnight. His blood test showed that one of his liver enzymes was raised and also, more worryingly, that his protein levels were dangerously low.

It was decided to let Lloyd come home the following afternoon and that we would continue to closely monitor the situation. That evening he ate some chicken and rice, his first meal with us. His mouth was still sore after losing all his teeth but he seemed to feel so much better without all that poison in his mouth. It began to worry me that Lloyd did not seem interested in drinking water. I tried different containers but he just would not touch it despite the warm weather.

We fed Lloyd on simple foods such as chicken, rice and scrambled eggs in an effort to resolve the problem of his faeces being so black and liquefied. I made sure he had plenty of chicken broth with his food to compensate for his reluctance to drink water. We returned to the vet five days later for a check and thankfully he was not dehydrated.

However, we became increasingly worried and decided to take a faecal sample to the vet for analysis. The results took a few days to come back from the lab. They revealed that he was suffering from Giardiasis, a parasitic infection of the bowel, and also Campylobacter. He was prescribed several drugs in an effort to combat these infections.
It is very likely that Lloyd had been suffering from them for some considerable time so it was not going to be easy to undo the harm that they might have caused. It is likely that poor quality drinking water plus sub-standard or infected food caused or contributed to the two diseases.

We desperately wanted to help Lloyd to get better. He was such a wonderful chap and became very attached to me in particular. This was due to the fact that he needed guidance around strange areas until he could find his way unaided. He had no sight at all but was a very determined boy. I would often discover that he had found his way from the hall out into the garden on his own, negotiating the kitchen and sun lounge as he went. He was so affectionate and we did want him to have some quality of life after such a miserable existence for so many years.

However, despite eating well and the treatment, he continued to suffer with his bowels. He also began to be nauseous. The vet advised us that the outlook was not good. There was every indication that his intestines had been damaged badly and that he could well be suffering from cancer. We decided to try a different treatment which can sometimes have good results. He was put on steroids combined with a new drug. We kept detailed records of everything he ate and the times when he had the drugs to make sure he was getting every chance for them to work.

Initially, the new treatment seemed to be working. Lloyd was more alert and interested in what was going on. He continued to enjoy his little walks and he appeared to be so happy in his home. He was so good with the other dogs in our care, such a friendly chap and utterly devoted to me in particular. He loved his cuddles and slept happily at the bottom of the bed on his own thick duvet and surrounding pillows to give him extra comfort. He was still so thin and bony. It was horrifying to see what an emaciated creature he was, yet still, we hoped and prayed that he would recover with the aid of the treatment. He was not ready to give up just when he had found a home of his own and while he was fighting we would do everything we could to help him win his battle for life.

Tragically, it was not to be. Our dear boy became weaker and we realised that his pathetic body had been too severely damaged to recover. He simply did not have the physical strength to fight, however much he desperately wanted to stay here. Maybe if he had come to us earlier and the treatment was started then, he would have had a fighting chance. It was too late for our boy. He had languished in kennels for many years since running his last race. He was forgotten about and ignored. He had not received the care which should have been his right.

At 1pm on the 12th August 2004, Lloyd died in my arms, on his duvet at the foot of my bed. He knew nothing as the vet slipped the needle into his leg. There was no movement or sound from him. He just slipped quietly out of this cruel world, which had done him no favours, until it was too late.

It is very hard to write about my boy as I miss him terribly and he is forever in my thoughts, despite the fact that I have since taken on yet another poorly old boy to join our family of eight dogs here at Tailends. It is heartbreaking to fail. Lloyd was here for just two months but in that time we became very close. I so wanted to give him some more time to enjoy the comfort of being cared for in a home with a friend who loved him and would make sure he never suffered or was neglected ever again. Wait for me Lloyd, with the growing family of dogs who we have loved and cared for and then had to lose. I cannot bear to think that we will never all meet again somewhere, one day. You deserved better in this world. I so hope you are now released from all the misery, loneliness and suffering that was inflicted on you by humans. I want to think of you with your eyes now, bright and clear, your body healthy with a shining coat and not a rib in sight. Dear Lloyd, a bit of me went with you that terrible day you left. You will never be forgotten.

Mark,

By Ami Barnikel, America

We met Mark shortly after one of my co-workers, who works with greyhound rescue in our area, sent a note to her work friends about the joys of adoption. We went online and saw his picture in the adoptable pets list. I immediately fell in love with him, just from his photo. And so did my kids, aged three and five. My husband however, was slow to warm up to the idea, telling us not to expect help caring for the dog from him.

Mark's story is scary and sad. The local rescue ranch owner, who helps turn out greys at the track kennels, found him. Mark's neck was slit open about six to eight inches across. No one seemed to know what had happened to him, so she took Mark to the vet and had him cared for. He was stitched up and recovered very nicely. He never lost his gentle demeanour or trust in people during the whole ordeal of injury, vet visits and recovery. He is still a gentle companion for my kids and me today.

And perhaps even more re"mark"ably, my husband has grown to love Mark too. He is the one who takes him for walks in the morning. And he is the one who has recently been reminding us that greys love the company of other greys, especially during the lonely days when their humans are away at school and work. So we are anxiously awaiting the day when we find a soul mate for Mark; a pretty little girl grey to complement his gentle and loving personality.

One Day With Maurice,

By Julie Hüwe, Germany

It was Christmas time when Nina, chairperson of *Greyhound Protection International (G.P.I.)*, asked me for help. While searching for a dog breed that would fit in to mine and my boyfriend's life, I had contacted *G.P.I.* a few months earlier and offered my help if it was ever needed. Back then I fell in love with the Spanish galgos and a few days before Christmas Eve, I found myself on the way to Frankfurt airport to pick up a young Galgo boy called Maurice.

Maurice was approximately eight months old. People had found him in the mountains around Granada with a severely injured paw, which is why part of one of his hind legs had to be amputated. The animal protectors wanted him to leave Spain as soon as possible. I had only seen some photographs of Maurice but he seemed like a very cute and handsome dog.

Even though I live in Cologne and Maurice was to come to Frankfurt, I decided that I would drive down to Frankfurt Airport to pick him up. I wanted him to be safe and well cared for. I did not bother about the distance or the time it would take for me to get him. Maurice's flight was scheduled for a Wednesday at 10:15 pm. I agreed to pick him up and take him to my place until *G.P.I.* would get him the next evening. This way I had a whole day to spend with the young boy, which I was looking forward to a lot!

I left Cologne at around 8 pm and drove to Frankfurt. The airport is easily accessible from the motorway and it was no problem to park my car in the underground car park of the respective terminal. The flight came in early but the dogs were the last ones to be unloaded. I waited for about half an hour until a young man came out with a huge box on his trolley. He was very nice and we had a quick chat about animal welfare and galgos before he handed me the vaccination document and the whole trolley with the box, which had the dog sitting inside. I guess the box was about four times bigger than the dog. I carefully pushed it into the elevator and went down to the parking deck. Before paying my parking ticket, I decided to open the box and introduce myself to Maurice. Also, I thought he might want to get out and move a little before he had to spend another two hours in my car. The little boy was very shy and couldn't be persuaded to relax a little and take a quick walk with me. He did not fancy food either, so I closed the box again, paid my ticket and pushed the trolley to my car. There Maurice had to leave the box. I gently pulled him out and put him down on his three legs. He was fine with that and walked around the car to the front-passenger seat. I lifted him onto the seat, which I had covered with old sheets and fixed the lead to the door handle. Now, while the dog was in the car starting to make himself comfortable, I was left with the box, which seemed to be too large to actually fit into the boot of my car.

It all worked out fine in the end and Maurice and I started heading back to Cologne. He managed to transform himself into a small pile that fitted the front-passenger seat and sat still, looking out of the window for the whole trip. On my arrival, my boyfriend was already waiting for us in front of the house. He took Maurice and walked with him to the nearest bush. The young Galgo peed immediately. We walked him for a couple of minutes and then carried him up to our flat on the third floor.

Maurice was pretty curious by then. He explored our place and started to follow us wherever we went. Both my boyfriend and I were very excited and observed every step he made. After a while we tried to settle him on a blanket in our bedroom. Maurice seemed to like his place but something was missing; a cuddly toy. First he chose my sheep doorstop, then my lamb shaped house-slippers and finally we surrendered our white toy seal to him. He took it and placed it next to his blanket where we found it untouched the next morning. The night was quiet. Maurice changed his position a couple of times and drank some water. He tried to join us in bed once but accepted that he couldn't join us there and finally fell asleep right next to our bed so we could all relax.

Early the next morning I made myself ready for a walk with Maurice. He got up and was excited the minute I sat up in bed. After a couple of minutes he was too excited to hold back any longer and peed on our floor; luckily he chose the laminate and not the carpet. Still, he behaved well on our walk and explored his new surroundings curiously. He could walk fine on his three legs and was interested in everything. Sometimes, when we met a big lorry, a train or a tram, he stopped and seemed a bit insecure about this loud and moving thing. However, as soon as the noisy something had passed he relaxed again and continued his discovery.

Maurice's first day in Germany consisted only of walking and being looked after. He quickly conquered the sofa and was lying on our lap for most of the time. He kept following us close enough to step on our shoes and seemed to enjoy himself.

In the evening it was already time to say goodbye to our new friend and I took him to an agreed place, to hand him over to Rosi and Marc from *G.P.I.* Maurice was to go to the society's place where all the dogs are kept for adoption. Rosi had to lift him out of my car and into theirs. Letting him go was pretty hard for me, even though I knew that Maurice would be fine and find a suitable family who would adopt him. I drove home knowing that I would pick up a galgo again any time and, more importantly, by that we would adopt one of these dogs as soon as possible.

Now, a few months later, it will not be long until a galgo will move in with us. My boyfriend and I are planning a trip to the *Scooby* animal home, in Spain, in March. We are confident to then find our new family member. And there is more good news. It seems that Maurice has found his new home! I wish him all the best and I am sure that Maurice and his new family will be happy together.

Mea, A Rescue Success Story,

By Kimberley Hall, America

One morning last February, a five month old Italian Greyhound was surrendered by her owners to the local humane society with a severely injured leg. Degloved by a raccoon trap, her leg was virtually unrecognizable and she was traumatized. The doctors worked diligently to save her leg but only time would tell if it would heal properly enough for her to use it. She spent four months in the hospital and by then all the staff knew that she was an amazing dog, who just needed to find an owner who would give her the love and attention that she deserved.

I am the owner of The Haute Hound, a luxury pet boutique in Jupiter. When I met Mea it was love at first site. I had worked closely with the humane society raising money for rescue at various events and already owned two Italian Greyhounds, called Rome and Sicily. The doctors wanted Mea to go to someone who knew the breed because she had special needs and would always require attention for her leg. I was an ideal choice. My dogs go to work with me and are rarely left alone. This was exactly what Mea needed.

I went to meet Mea for the first time after she had been in the hospital for two months. It was heartbreaking to see her leg all mangled and raw and her foot swollen almost three times its normal size. Mea was so timid and shy and hid her head on the staff member's chest the whole time, allowing me to pet her only a few times.

A month later, I brought my two dogs to meet Mea. She was just as shy as before; cowering and quite unsure what to do as Sicily and Rome gave her a thorough sniffing. After they both decided she was acceptable, they went on to sniffing other things. Only then did Mea move out to sniff them. Finally, a breakthrough!

One month later, Mea was ready to go home! Her leg was covered in scars and a three-inch long section was missing fur and muscle that would never grow back. The leg wouldn't bend and one toe and the pad on the bottom were missing. Mea was a very lucky girl to still have use of this leg at all. Having left the girls at home, I picked her up one bright sunny day in May and what a happy day it was. The first time I took her to the dogpark, Mea never left my lap. Now four months later, Mea is the queen of the dogpark. She runs around chasing all the other dogs and even gives her sisters a run for their money. She will then lounge contentedly on the grass after tiring herself out, everything alright with the world.

Once Mea settled in, I noticed that when moving around she would fling her leg about and usually ended up hitting someone with it by accident. Because the nails on the three remaining toes stick straight out, I named her foot, "The Claw!" Mea reigns supreme over this household brandishing of "The Claw!" whenever she deems it is necessary.

Mea loves to chase the cat around the house. She has learned to sit, loves treats, and plays with her toys like they are going out of style, especially her rubber chicken. But her favorite pastimes are receiving kisses on the sides of her face and cuddling with her mom. To get to me, Mea has no qualms about walking right over her sisters to do it. She is quite a character! I've never had a dog make me laugh as much as Mea does. I never know what she's going to do next and she's so smart!

Sometimes, being that smart gets Mea into trouble. She has figured out how to get treats off the table and steals toys out of the toy bin at my pet boutique. If I see her sprinting off towards the backroom of the store then I know something's up. But when Mea gives me that sweet, beguiling look, I can never stay mad.

Rescue dogs really do know that you've given them a second chance at life and they are forever expressing their appreciation for it. I love all my dogs madly, but when I look at Mea, my heart swells because I know she's been through so much and yet is able to maintain her optimism and sheer enjoyment of life. We all could take a lesson from her. I'm so glad that she came into my life.

Molly,

By Patty Hopkins, America

Our greyhound Molly came to us in a most unexpected way. We were at Semoran Skateway for an eleventh birthday party for one of my daughters. This just happened to be the same day as a *Greyhound Ranch* "Meet & Greet" was held there. Upon entering the lobby of the skating rink, my husband was immediately drawn to these graceful, sweet natured dogs. Throughout the two hours we were there we both kept going back, time and time again, to pet them and enjoy those leaning greyhound hugs. Neither of us had ever met a retired racer before and we were in awe of their beauty and calm demeanour.

That day, one dog in particular was memorable for us. Dear sweet Molly, who was a little shy at first, was a beautiful brindle, with a white collar, who also had some serious scars on her back. Rumour had it that these were the result of a beating by her trainer. Our heart went out to her at that very moment and we could not get her out of our thoughts.

It was a short two weeks later that Molly came for a home visit and never left. Our eleven year old German Short Hair, Maggie, was like a kid at Christmas. She was so excited to have a new canine friend. It was precious to see. They were fast friends from the moment they met.

We weren't sure if Molly was "cat friendly" as she had never had a feline friend, but it turned out that our cat Charley set her straight very soon on who was "boss" of the house. They now coexist peacefully and it is apparent Molly has not a mean bone in her body.

We fenced in our half an acre side yard for Molly and Maggie and every day we are treated to watching that famous greyhound run. It is a joy to see. It warms our heart to think that we have given a retired racer a happy life and we are daily getting so very much love in return. We see many more greyhounds in our future!

A true Princess

Billy, a prize winner now!

Ami, centre, with her greyhound family

Bessie-poetry in motion

Blue Bob - a raving lunatic!

Bonnie Cole, a true survivor

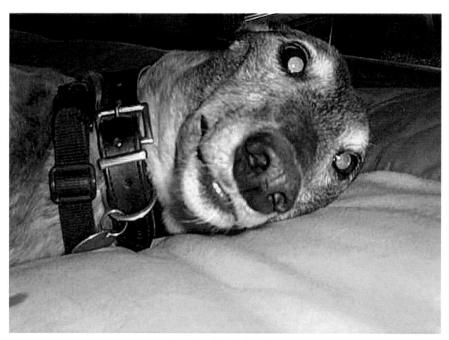

Cassi, with a big grin

Connor leading the way, with his brother Mike behind

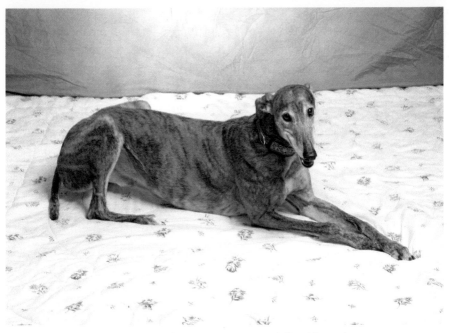

Frankie, A perfect gentleman, especially with cats!

Isabella who flew all the way from Spain to the U.S.A

Jagger, a miraculous recovery thanks to his devoted owners

Jessie, otherwise as "Jessie Jumble" or "Fangs"

Judy, with her loving owner Mike

Lloyd, a dear boy

Mark, a gentle companion

Mea, queen of the dogpark

Bonnie, a dear old lady

Paddy, the adventurer

Amazing Grace

Scooby, a loving dog, twenty four seven

Scotts Kelly, a "Pets As Therapy" dog

Sheri, a gorgeous girl

Snowy, so caring for her canine and human family

Trek and Ryhndda, waiting for Aunty Mary

My Dogs,

By Margaret Gomm, Wales

Until a few years ago, I had over thirty lurchers, all rescued and each with a story. They ranged in size from almost as large as greyhounds to whippet size.

Sinbad was a large lurcher who I had to have put to sleep in 2004, because he had cancer. He was twelve and a half. He had been left neglected and shut in a shed for nearly three years. He was starved, had skin rash, fleas and wasn't socialised with humans. Once he got settled with me, he loved company but hated if a visitor got up to leave. He would run to the door to prevent them going out. He was very insecure and destructive, as rescued dogs often are, and would rip things up if he was left alone. My car was stripped back to the metal and I have had to have new seat belts as the lurchers have chewed them up over the years.

I have helped many other dogs. On one occasion I went to a car boot and saw a large man, with a stick, hitting a lurcher who was very thin. His little ribs stuck out. I felt his pain. I tackled this man over his cruelty and the little dog's eyes were looking at me, asking me to help him. The man and I had words. I offered to buy the dog but he wouldn't part with him, because he had caught six rabbits and was valuable to him for this.

During the day, I kept an eye on the guy. The little dog's eyes seemed to be pleading for help. I wrote down the vehicle registration and tried to trace the man. I wondered how many other dogs he owned. I had given him my phone number in the hope he would contact me if he changed his mind. I had nightmares seeing the dog's eyes asking me for help.

Two weeks went by and then came a knock on the door. I went outside and saw the dog tied to a tree in front of my house and very ill. He is around nine years old now, with an enlarged heart so we take it one day at a time.

My Trip To The Greyhound Race Track,

By F.J., aged 11, Scotland

My mum, sister and I went to Northern Ireland for the weekend. My mum finds out things about greyhound racing and what happens so she can try and stop it. Mum hates greyhound racing because of all the dogs that suffer and die.

We live with lots of greyhounds at home and I like them, although they take up the couch and don't behave sometimes. Mum says this is because of how they are treated when they race. I know that there are too many greyhounds and not enough homes like ours for them, which means that some of them die. That makes me sad.

Mum said we were going to one of the greyhound tracks in Northern Ireland, called Ballyskeagh, near Belfast. We went and pretended that we liked it and bet on it but we didn't. I felt a bit scared because I didn't know what would happen.

We got to the parking lot and Mum stopped the car. Mum gave the man 20p so we could park. The man taking the money was tall and thin and he had a yellow jacket on. He looked a bit strange but let us go through and there were lots of cars. The building was tall with graffiti on the outside wall and we got out of the car and walked to the entrance.

There were two men who were waiting there and we paid them £5 for Mum and they let my sister and I go in free. We walked through the entry bit and out into the stadium. I looked around and there were lots of people. I started to become really sad as I hated being there. There were lots of men shouting and swearing, especially at the men taking bets. Who would be silly enough to bet on a living dog?

I sat down on a dirty blue chair. The stadium was big and dirty and quite scary. There was a football pitch in the middle. Mum said that it was a greyhound racing track as well as a football pitch.

Mum asked me to go to the barrier and look at the sand. I did and I could see the concrete underneath it. Mum said that the man who owned the track had fallen out with some people and couldn't get anyone to sell him sand. She also told me that one of our dogs at home had broken her leg at this track and that made me very sad.

I heard a horn of some kind being blown and the shouting with the men and the bets stopped. The dogs looked terrible. They were thin and you could see their bones; not like my own dogs. I stood over beside the cages that they put them in at the start and some of the men were quite rough, pushing them in and closing the door. The dogs looked sad. I started to worry about them.

When they were in the hatches, the rabbit came zooming round and the hatch opened and out came the dogs. I knew what went on after this. The dogs ran round the track and people started shouting. It was minging. The people were shouting and swearing at the dogs. It was terrible. We stayed for seven races.

I was scared about one of the dogs who came last and quite a bit behind the other dogs. I also heard one of them scream after being knocked over by another dog while they were running.

My sister, who is six, nearly gave us away by getting quite upset and saying loudly that she thought it was cruel. We went to the toilets and stuck some stickers on the doors. Mum said that it was wrong but this time she wouldn't ground me!

We went out to the car and drove off. I hated it. I am scared that some of these dogs will die now. Mum said that in Northern Ireland greyhounds die every day. I know they die here too but more of them die over there when they can no longer run. When I got home I cuddled my greyhounds hard.

Our Dear Old Lady, Bonnie,

By Angela Hogan, England

It was the 24th January, 2002, when we first met Bonnie. She shared our home for just twenty-one months but in that time she touched our lives in a very special way.

Bonnie had spent her early life as a racing greyhound, serving her owners by running her heart out for them on the track as they had trained her to do. When Bonnie was about six years old she was considered no longer fast enough to race and was retired. However, there was no loving home, or cosy fireside in winter, for Bonnie. She was left in the kennels where she had lived during her working life. Her life for the next six years was bleak and loveless. She was never taken out for a walk but remained in her kennel as the seasons changed. In the summer it was often very hot and her kennel was smelly. Her owner often forgot to give her any fresh water to drink and she was constantly thirsty.

However, it was the winter which really caused the most suffering for this poor creature. She was fed on very basic food, which usually consisted only of stale bread soaked in water. When it rained the wind blew the sheets of saturating icy wetness through her kennel. There was no protection from it and nowhere to escape the cold and wet. Her meagre rations gave her no chance to build up any resistance against these brutal conditions. The stench from the lack of hygiene would horrify anyone with any compassion for these poor dogs. The roof of her kennel leaked and her bed was wet and filthy. She stood in her own urine and excrement and waited for death, which would have been a blessed release for this poor helpless girl. Nobody ever came and gave her a pat or a kind word. The kennel owner had lots of other dogs to look after and many were still racing. There was no time for Bonnie. There was no warm heated kennel, no fleecy coat to wear when she was cold. We will never know how she survived these years of hardship and misery; perhaps by retreating within herself more and more as the years passed.

Greyhounds have a capacity for putting up with the most dreadful neglect and yet they bear no malice towards their human jailers.

Christmas 2001 was the time when poor Bonnie could not cope any longer. She had become so thin that she could hardly stand. Thankfully, there were a few people involved with the welfare of greyhounds who were aware of the problems in this kennel. They managed to get the owner to agree to hand Bonnie over to them. She was by this time nearly twelve years old and extremely confused.

We take in dogs which are unlikely to find homes in the normal way, due to old age or health problems, although space determines how many we can accommodate at any one time. When we heard about Bonnie we desperately wanted to give this poor girl some home comforts for her last months on this earth. We wanted her to know that life could be good and that there was someone who would love her and protect her; all things she had never known.

On the 24th January, Bonnie was driven to Bristol, where we made her comfortable in our car for the last part of her journey to our coastal home in North Devon. She was painfully thin and did not seem to want to eat, despite being offered all sorts of appetising food. Her eyes had a glazed expression as if she had given up on life. They seemed to say she did not care what happened to her now and that death would be welcome. We tempted her to eat by putting food on our fingers and gently pushing them in her mouth. Soon she was responding and seemed surprised to find that eating could be a pleasurable experience. It was not long before she was eating from a bowl full of tasty food. She was fond of scrambled eggs so this was on the menu for breakfast daily. She also loved cheese. This would not normally be a good choice for an old dog but she needed to put on some fat and she did enjoy it so much that we made sure she had some with her food most days. Gradually, she really began to look forward to meal times and seemed delighted at all the new tastes she was experiencing for the first time.

As time passed, Bonnie changed from the pathetic creature we had seen when she arrived, into a beautiful, happy, affectionate lady. Her quality of life improved tremendously after our vet removed thirteen rotten teeth, which had decayed through years of poor nutrition. She could now eat firmer food and treats, which she so enjoyed.

Bonnie trusted us implicitly. She never flinched as the other dogs rushed out of the room when the vacuum cleaner came out. She knew we would never harm her and she had no need to be afraid of anything so long as we were there to protect her. Gradually she started to really enjoy her walks along the beach and dunes. Soon she got used to the walking routine and would get so excited when it was nearly time to go out. She used to do a little dance, jumping around in a circle and dropping down on her front legs, giving little barks. The other dogs were a bit bemused by this strange behaviour but they never seemed to mind when she barked at them in glee. We realised that she was probably quite confused in her mind as a result of her former treatment but we know she was happy and was delighted to be a part of our little family; a very special part. The love she gave to us was something different to anything we had known before.

On the sixteenth of October, Bonnie seemed a bit wheezy and nauseous. The vet said her chest had a little rattle and she had a chest infection. She was put on antibiotics and within a few days, she was back to normal. However, on Thursday, October 30th, 2003, Bonnie was slightly hesitant to go out for the afternoon walk and I decided to leave her at home. She did not want to be left though, so came after us, asking to have her coat on and come with the others. Later that afternoon, she had her dinner in the normal way and spent a quiet night sleeping at the bottom of our bed on her quilt as usual. The next day Bonnie did not get up to go on the early walk but just remained sleeping on her bed. When I tried to take her along to the field for a short walk on my return, she still did not want to get up and I began to get worried. We decided to take her to the vet immediately. She got up as we put our coats on and walked to the car, where we gently lifted her in. The vet listened to her chest and found that her heartbeat was very muffled on one side. She was concerned and decided to keep Bonnie in for X-rays to determine what exactly was going on.

Later that morning the vet rang to say that Bonnie had an aggressive cancer in her lungs. We were devastated, as we were not prepared for such news. It had all happened so quickly. The vet said that we could take Bonnie home for a few days on drugs if we really wanted to, but, that her advice would be to let her go then. She said that she might become unable to breathe and become very distressed. We drove back to the vet and asked to go straight to the recovery area where Bonnie was sleeping on her blanket.

I saw at once that she had deteriorated further since we left her earlier that day. She showed no sign of pain but was gradually slipping away. I knelt down beside her and she opened her eyes and raised her head slightly so I knew she was aware that her mum was with her. I cuddled her in my arms for the last time and asked if the vet could just let her go there, rather than move her to the surgery. I noticed no movement or even the slightest quiver as she let go of her hold on life. Our dear girl had gone from this world, where she had suffered so much. We can only be grateful that we were able to give her some of the love and care that was absent from the greater part of her life.

Who is responsible for the suffering of this poor girl? Is it the trainer who owned her and chose to keep her in inadequate kennels after her racing career was finished? Or is it the industry that creates the problem in the first place? Should this business, which makes so much money from these loyal loving animals, not accept complete responsibility for each and every dog that is bred for it, whether they actually retire or are one of the thousands which are not suitable for racing and never even reach a track? With very few exceptions, rescues throughout this country have greyhounds looking for homes in addition to the other unwanted and homeless dogs. Is it not time the racing industry accepted their responsibility for these dogs and not leave it to others to pick up and care for the "trash" from their lucrative business?

The most unbearable fact in this story is not the sad death of our dear Bonnie, (who we mourn daily) but that there are others like her, thousands of them. Some are as yet unborn but will suffer similar fates, maybe without the care and love that she had in her last months. The kennel Bonnie lived in is still full of dogs and there are many others that are even worse. Some dogs are neglected and are the victims of ignorance while others are deliberately abused and ill-treated. They are just seen as an expendable commodity to many in the racing world. There are some trainers who are excellent and their dogs have the best of care and are looked after very well even when they are retired, but this is not good enough.

Every dog has a right to have an acceptable level of care throughout his life, even if he is to spend it within a kennel. This is a country of severe dog overpopulation and yet the racing industry adds to the already overwhelming problem. It would be statistically impossible for every dog bred for racing to be looked after properly throughout his life. There are simply not enough suitable homes available and there would never be room for the quantity of good kennels needed or the resources available to ensure that the standards were of an acceptable level. I cannot be at peace while I know that dogs are still suffering like our dear girl did, literally buried in unknown hellholes, hidden from public view. I can see no solution and no end to the suffering while greyhound racing continues in its present form. I would like to pay tribute to those whose commitment and sacrifice has helped to give some greyhounds a better life. Without them many more dogs would have been killed or left to live out a miserable existence.

Paddy,

By Emma Burke, England

We had always had dogs at home as children, so when I left my Mum's house to live on my own, I decided I wanted a dog. It was November 1988 and I was looking through a copy of the *Liverpool Echo* when an advert caught my eye; 'Good homes wanted for unwanted dogs.' I rang the number and spoke to a lady who reeled off a list of dogs. Amongst them was a sixteen - week old greyhound, Callum. His mother had had Parvo virus and had just had puppies in a racing kennel in Liverpool. The owner had the mother put to sleep and all the pups had died, apart from this one, and he was very poorly. The vet told the owner that he was hoping the puppy would make a full recovery, but because he had been so ill he would not be strong enough to race. When the owner heard this he said, "Oh, I'm not interested then..." and walked out of the surgery. The nurses then looked after the puppy and paid for his treatment from their own money. He was on a drip for five weeks and had to be turned over regularly to prevent blood clots.

When he was close to recovery he was put up for adoption, which is when I homed him and called him 'Paddy.' He was like a little skeleton. He had to have fish, rice and eggs and other bland food for weeks until he was better. Even now he loves fried rice from the Chinese take away. He was very weak and it took a while for him to fully recover. Now, he's ten and a half years old and showing signs of age, such as grey hair. He doesn't seem to be slowing down much, apart from the odd bout of cramp or stiffness after a good run. In the past ten years I have had lots of ups and downs in my life and Paddy has always been with me, every step of the way. He is extremely determined, he knows exactly what he wants and usually makes sure he gets it! Paddy is very clever and has done some amusing (and amazing) things in his time.

On one occasion he barked during the night to go out for a wee so I let him out. Unbeknown to me he squeezed through a tiny gap in the fence and after having a nosy round, set off for my Mum's house.

My mum was fast asleep. He stood at the front of her house, barking and looking up to the bedroom window as if to say "I'm here !" This was at about 4.30am. This may not seem that amazing but I actually lived about four miles away from my Mum at this time! I would have loved to know if the route he took was the same one I used to drive. The only thing I can think of is that, months earlier, it was a Bank Holiday Monday and I was bored, so we walked to my Mum's house. I wonder if he followed this scent even though it was ages after? Only Paddy knows!

Sadly, since Paddy's story was written, he has passed away, but we wanted to include his story in memory of this very special greyhound.

Allegory of Phantom,

By Ann Merriam, England

Phantom was born with an internal drive for freedom. This freedom would take her through being constantly hunted, subject to terrible punishment of body from cold and storms, being pregnant and the loss of pups, threatened in quest of food, prey to insects and parasites and lacking the of comfort of love. This drive eventually sealed her death. Only after she was forced into total surrender was she to receive a year's gift of human bounty, care, and love; things she had unknowingly sacrificed for freedom.

It took humans with remarkable commitment, resources, persistence, and love to be the rescuing hunters. They had to match wits and endurance of cold and storms; they had to sacrifice travel and vet expense; they dealt with sometimes obstructive local authorities but they continued through discouraging defeats. As Phantom came close to death for freedom, her hunters risked their own lives by tracking her with antenna in a lightning storm.

After her capitulation and immediate medical attention, Phantom was adopted into a life of the best of care, physically, happily, and lovingly. She died very suddenly at home, which was probably an unavoidable result of treatment for parasites acquired in her feral life. Her rescuers grieve that she could not have longer to enjoy the extent of the human care and love that she would die to escape from. Her rescuers do not regret the risks and efforts made to allow her even so short taste of a cherished animal's life.

Greyhound Puppy Auctions,

By Olga Ferguson and Amanda Wells, Scotland

Representatives from *Greyhound Action Scotland* and *Advocates for Animals* travelled to Dublin, from Edinburgh, to attend the greyhound sales at Harold's Cross Stadium. At the airport we met up with an independent greyhound and lurcher rescuer from the south of England. On arrival at the stadium car park, the first thing that struck me was the appearance of some of the men hanging about. Let's just say you wouldn't want to meet them in a dark alley! Secondly, I noticed the vehicles parked there with small, metal trailers hitched to the back of them, used for transporting greyhounds. I thought this was a pretty awful mode of transport for the dogs. It transpires that dogs have been known to die in these trailers from car exhaust fumes. Other greyhounds were in estate car boots, or in crates in the back of vans.

The lorry that one of these men allegedly uses for transporting greyhounds to the Barcelona track in Spain, a fairly small white lorry with a navy blue covering, was also there and we parked next to it. His main job is as a transporter of dogs to England for flapping tracks, but he is the only person who will transport dogs to Spain taking thirty six small bitches crammed into his van with no water, or food, or climate control, or proper stops for all that distance. Despite the combined *I.S.P.C.A. & R.S.P.C.A.* operation where the police stopped him, he is still transporting dogs to Spain in these conditions.

Cheap, small bitches are selected. They have to be small, so that they can get round the notoriously tight bends of the track at Barcelona. They are cheap because they are a disposable form of entertainment. The quality of the racing is not appreciated in Spain, just the entertainment value and the betting.

No notification of who buys what is given after the greyhound sales. Quite frequently, the customs and officials at the ferry ports do not even know that this man has a load of dogs in the lorry, because the dogs are so heavily drugged prior to transport that they do not make a sound.

At the stadium that day, several men were standing about with their greyhounds. I was struck by the relatively small amount of people there; there couldn't have been more than a hundred or so at the sales. The people were virtually all male; the few women there stood out. They seemed a mostly older age group (fifty plus) of rough looking Irish men. There were some more smartly dressed men as well, and a few fathers there, who had taken sons, as young as five years old, along. They were all there to buy and sell dogs.

Apart from our Rescue contact, who blended in posing as a buying trainer and got chatting to a few people, nobody tried to speak to us, although being a group of women, we must have stood out like a sore thumb.

One little old woman with a huge greyhound appeared. She said she was training him for someone who races at Sunderland track. We all started petting him. She seemed a little perturbed by the fact that we were paying so much attention to him and said, 'He doesn't get that at home' quite seriously. That was obvious to us.

We wandered into the kennel block, where the dogs are held before and after racing, to have a look. There were small, individual kennels, the size of fairly small crates, made of solid metal, with small holes in the front door for ventilation. They reminded me of cloakroom lockers. Apparently, these are good kennels by the standards of many racetracks.

We bought a programme, which we would mark up during the trials, trying to identify which bitches may be sent to Spain from these sales. We hung around next to the track for a while, where groups of men and dogs were standing about in small clusters. None of these dogs displayed any of the excitement that the racers so often speak of.

How many times have we heard the phrases "The dogs love racing; you should see their excitement when you pull up at the track, take them out of the car and they know that they're going to race!" There was no evidence of this. What struck me most profoundly throughout the day was the complete lack of emotion in both the dogs and the people.

Of course, there were a few exceptions but the majority of dogs were 'glazed over'; numb, glassy eyed, quiet, detached and shut-off. Anyone who has an adopted greyhound will have seen this 'numbness' in their new dog for the first few weeks. This is exactly what they were like at the track too. The men paid no attention to the dogs at all, not even to check them over prior to the trials. They were completely ignored, with no interaction or petting. There was no interaction or acknowledgement between the various groups of dogs either; if they so much as look at each other on the track, they are disqualified for 'fighting'. It was a bitterly cold day, but throughout the day, of the over a hundred dogs that were there, I counted around five wearing kennel coats or jackets to keep them warm.

The trials began. Over a hundred greyhounds ran. For some reason, there were never more than four running in each trial and in a couple of trials toward the end of different distances, only two running against each other. The dogs get one trial each to prove their ability. One of the buyers remarked that Harold's Cross was a bad track with tight bends and if a dog can run here, it can run anywhere.

As the dogs were led across the concourse and approached the traps, most just walked along with their owners like automatons. A few seemed reluctant to get into the trap and were pushed in. Once out of the traps, they all ran of course.

There were so many dogs but a few stand out in my memory.
One near the beginning was very, very slow; she must've been about twenty lengths behind the other dogs, all the way round the track. I felt worried about that dog and was looking out for her at the sale, but she had been withdrawn, due to running so badly, I suppose. The other that I remember was a tiny black bitch. She was so small. She came in last.

Several times, the dogs seemed to slip and almost fall at the first bend; eventually, one fell. The spectators gasped. He picked himself back up and continued running. They usually get up again and keep running, especially if they only have minor injuries. Occasionally, even with broken limbs, they sometimes keep running, because they are

concentrating so hard on the race. After the trial, the dog's owner
was checking him over for injuries. I do not know if there was any
vet in attendance at these trials. Certainly, no one else appeared at
the trackside to look at the dog. A few other dogs seemed to run in an
odd way; one not putting any pressure on a hind leg; one with a
bent tail.

Whilst we were watching the trials, we got chatting to two buyers
sitting near us; a father and son, both Dubliners. The son had been
coming to the sales since he was five years old and now owned several
racing dogs, which he kept in a shed in his garden. He didn't look more
than seventeen years old, but as our Rescue contact remarked: "Owning
greyhounds is like owning socks over here".

The trials over, after a break for lunch, the auction began. There was
an auction room in the stadium; a ring space where the dogs are led out
individually by one of the two track handlers for 'viewing', whilst men
seated on wooden benches or standing at the ringside bid on them. It
was a horrible thing seeing the first few being sold like poor cows, but
after the first few, my mind just shut off and became numb, until the
terrified dogs came into the ring.

A small handful of the dogs, about half a dozen maybe, appeared
confident and happy; the vast majority were blank and dazed looking;
several were terrified by this experience. One small brindle bitch, Bo,
freaked out when the steward went to check her ear tattoo. She reared
up and twisted back, desperately trying to get away. She was extremely
hand-shy. The only person in the entire place who seemed to show any
kindness toward the dogs was one of the lead-outs; a young lad, who
tried to reassure the frightened dogs with a pat on the head, but to little
avail. Some of these scared dogs had to be virtually dragged into the
ring, and were pulled into a kind of sitting position, since they did not
want to budge. The brindle bitch cowered and no one bid on her.
Distressed by Bo's fear, we tried to negotiate with the owner outside
to purchase her, but he insisted on €150 and wouldn't take less. We
couldn't pay that, but spoke again to the young lad whom we had met
during the trials. He had wanted to bid on the dog but his father had

stopped him. He then went and bought the brindle bitch privately from the owner and we were relieved that she, at least, would not go to Barcelona and was with one of the 'better' ones. Subsequently, she was sold again at Peterborough auctions in April.

There was a series of dogs, two brindles and several black ones, which seemed very nervous in the ring; shaking, cowering, with heads and tails right down. Some of these were bought, some not. With some of the unsold dogs, either because no-one bid or the reserve wasn't met, deals are done 'privately' outside the auction room. Dogs and money change hands in the car park.

The Dublin sales are supposedly the most prestigious in Ireland! We had bid on the dog that had fallen at his trial. We were the only bidder but the reserve was not met by a €100 bid. We do not know what happened to him. The cheapest dogs went for around €150 and the most expensive €2200. The average price was around €300. Apparently, the dogs were much dearer than at previous Dublin sales that our contacts had attended, where many went for €50 in the sale room and as little as €10 in the car park. No wonder they are so disposable.

The black greyhounds, currently an unfashionable colour amongst the racers, are referred to as 'bin-liners,' because they are black and so disposable. At one point, I overheard a conversation between a man and a very respectable looking middle-aged lady seated behind us. The lady's husband was selling one of their dogs, which had made €700. The man asked "Are you happy with that then?" She replied "Oh yes, very pleased". I was struck by the complete business-like callousness of this whole thing. One feels she might have been a more upset if she had sold a family heirloom or favourite antique at auction, but there were no such feelings for a living, breathing, feeling dog.

We noted several Scottish buyers there. A group of three men had been sitting behind us on the outbound flight from Edinburgh and had come to the sales. They purchased five dogs for flapping that would be taken to Edinburgh by a transporter guy who only transports dogs to Scotland.

Eventually, the sale ended. Most of the buyers had left around two thirds of the way through and in hindsight, I wish some of us had stayed in the car park to see what was going on there. When we got to the car park, almost all the trailers and transporters had gone and all that was left were several Mercedes Benz luxury saloons.

All I kept thinking about during the auction was the dogs and imagining my own greyhounds being traded like this. We went back to the airport, feeling drained. At the time, it was not as distressing as I had expected it to be, but subsequently, the image of all those dogs kept going through my mind; wondering where they'll end up, how they will be treated and what will happen to them next.

I left the sales with a real sense of how there are just so many cheap dogs that are seen as 'worthless' by the racing community. Worthless because they are not of high monetary value and worthless because they are just racing machines to them, not dogs. At this sale, I really got no sense or impression of a great love for the dogs themselves that some talk of. It was plain to see the truth of the matter that we all knew before hand; that in Ireland, where the vast majority are bred and reared, greyhounds are regarded as 'live-stock'.

A couple of days later, I was walking my greyhounds when a stranger approached me, asking first if they were 'rescue' dogs. When I replied 'yes,' he patted one and explained to me that his son had a rescue greyhound. He remarked, "It takes a long time to get any emotion out of them. It's a shame really, isn't it?

In the meantime, under the guise as a potential greyhound racing dog owner, we kept in touch with one of the Irish racing people. It transpired that his business was to buy greyhounds cheaply in Dublin and bring them over to the UK sales where he would make quite a profit. We discovered that the next sales would be at Peterborough Stadium on Good Friday. I met up with our rescue contact and went along.

My 'disguise' was as someone who had become interested in greyhounds and was looking to buy one to run at Shawfield stadium. We met up almost immediately with our contacts who were selling on the greyhounds that had been bought at Harold's Cross. We managed to obtain quite a bit of information about what goes on behind the scenes.

The crowd was completely different to Dublin. We entered the stadium and went into the restaurant/viewing area. No one was able to go outside and see the greyhounds. It was fairly busy inside. Fortunately we managed to get closer to the front and sat with the Irish 'sellers'. We had marked out the greyhounds we had concerns about – in particular Bo, who was the brindle bitch who was terrified at Dublin. The son of the Irish seller had been working with her and he told us she was coming along well; her problem with her nerves had improved and she was now racing better.

We were introduced to a guy, hereafter referred to as "X", who came over from Ireland and his business was to buy in Ireland and re-sell in England. All of the greyhounds auctioned were described as 'direct from Ireland,' therefore they had all been brought over in the previous days, specifically to be auctioned to race at UK tracks.

The trials over, after a break for lunch, the auction began. Unlike Dublin, the auctioneer came to the front of the restaurant and the greyhounds were brought out onto the track, therefore you could only view them from a distance. The auction itself appeared more humane than it did in Dublin, but that may have been because we weren't close enough to see the greyhounds fear.

The first greyhound I was looking out for was our Bo. If need be I was prepared to bid for her. However, as she had vastly improved, she was bid for and sold at £400. I was relieved. Although she will now enter racing, she is safe for the next year or so. My main fear was that she would be 'disposed of' if she wasn't sold. In sterling, Bo had been bought at Dublin for £100, which means a 300% profit was made on her sale. The seller had around ten greyhounds for auction that day and managed to sell all of them.

Our Irish seller had put word out that I was a new greyhound owner and was looking for a greyhound to race in Scotland. The other Irish seller, X, approached me. He said to me that he had a black greyhound bitch that would be ideal for the Scottish tracks, in particular the flapping tracks. He said she takes the bends well. It turned out that she had been up for auction but no one had bid for her. He was your traditional Irish charmer and he said he would let me have her for £150. I said I would think about it. He came to me a few times before the auction ended and asked if I had thought about it, at one point practically sitting on my knee to 'charm' me into buying her. I tried to act in a non-committal way.

We asked our Irish seller what happens to the greyhounds that don't get sold. He said that if they had potential, they would be taken back with him and auctioned after some work had been put in to improve their performance. He didn't answer what happened if they had no potential. However, we did get back to that subject and he admitted that they would be destroyed, probably by shooting before they boarded the ferry. He told us that X would do the same. He claims that it costs 250 Euros to have a greyhound put to sleep in the South so it would simply been too expensive to take a 'useless' greyhound back.

The highest priced greyhound sold for about £3500 and the lowest about £130 with varying prices in between. Three guys sitting in front of us bid for and bought several of the higher priced hounds.

Two of the greyhounds that hadn't met their reserve bids went back up for auction. Neither reached the price that they had previously been bid at and rejected. The sellers began to debate with the auctioneer who simply ended the sale. My own impression of that scenario was that the auctioneer was unhappy at their last ditch attempt to sell these greyhounds rather than take them back to Ireland. I felt they were just greedy. At the end several people hung around to pay off what they owed for the greyhounds.

Afterwards, I managed to get inside the kennel block. When the individual kennel was opened, it appeared that there was no lighting or natural light at all inside the kennel, which measured about three foot by four. The kennel had 'paper' bedding for the hounds to lie in. Although I wasn't expecting high quality kennelling, I did expect there to be some kind of lighting for the dogs, although it does explain why one of my rescued racing dogs hates being in the dark.

X came after me as we were walking to the van in the car park. He brought with him the little black greyhound bitch. He turned on the charm and again offered her to me for £150. I bartered with him and managed to get him down to £100. To be honest I would have paid ten times that amount for her because I knew her alternative was certain death. I also managed to negotiate the collar and lead, as I didn't have a spare one.

I realise that I was potentially funding him to continue with his trade in greyhounds, but I would have found it impossible to walk away as most non-racing greyhound people would.

He asked me back to the kennels to pick up her stud card that lists her races, age and all other relevant information. He said that I would need a 'change of ownership' form. As a 'greyhound racing dog owner' I said I did. He went off again and returned with a form, which was all folded up saying that he'd filled it in and signed it.

X said to me that she's a good little runner. Yes, it was a dog he was referring to, not a car. He said if I sell her I should make sure I got a good price for her. He also said she'd make a good brood bitch once she'd finished racing. I nodded and smiled at him thinking how much I would like to tell him what I was doing there and that this little bitch had run her last ever race and would be neutered by the end of the week. But I held my tongue, smiled sweetly and we drove away.

We looked at the change of ownership form in the van. It was blank! I'm not really surprised that he did that but I wished I'd checked it before we'd left. I also looked at the stud card and discovered she wasn't coming up to two as it said in the auction catalogue, but actually coming up for three and nearing the end of her career. Having been in a situation before similar to this, I know that greyhound owners aren't always honest with their paperwork.

When I got her back to the hotel, she didn't do much other than look frightened. I saw that she was dirty and there appeared to be flea dirt on her. She was very frightened and lay down against the wall. She seemed to be watching me all the time but she obviously didn't trust me one bit. I phoned home and we came up with a name, Saorca, which is Gaelic for 'freedom'. It seemed appropriate!

The next day I left Peterborough. On route was a lady who I know and trust implicitly. She runs a greyhound rescue and I have a huge amount of respect for her and her opinion, as well as the work she does with 'rescued' greyhounds. I refuse to call any of them 'retired' now, because how can you possibly 'retire' in your prime? I dropped in to show Saorca to her and to check her over for any obvious illness or injury. However, my friend had kennel space so offered to take her in. She knew that if Saorca came home with me as a foster dog she wouldn't go any further, as I fail badly at fostering greyhounds and they always end up staying! So we agreed that she would stay and be re-homed from there, after being neutered.

Meanwhile, my friend renamed her Brenna, as the pronunciation of Saorca down there sounds like "saucer"! As it happens Brenna found a new home within only ten days in the North of Scotland! In contrast, my friend has another bitch who has been there eight months. Some greyhounds find homes quickly, others take forever. Brenna was and is lucky, but what happens to the next one, where there isn't someone like me to take her away and someone like my friend, who took her in and found her a forever home?

We followed through from the auctions at Dublin to the Peterborough sales. As far as I know none of the greyhounds bought at Peterborough would be taken back to auction, but they would begin their racing career from there. I decided that this was as far as I could take it. I am finding it increasingly difficult to be 'undercover' and smile sweetly, when in reality I have violent thoughts towards these people.

I have all the auctioned greyhounds' racing names and I will be tracking them in coming months to see where they are racing.

My one relief is that one of them has escaped from the awful world that is greyhound racing. I also recognise that these dogs are commodities and 'worthless'. I do believe that it's these people that miss out on seeing what the real qualities of a greyhound are.
I struggle with these dogs that show their fear or dead souls through their eyes. They have no reason to trust any human after the lives they have led, which may not be physical abuse in a broad sense of the word, but neglecting a dog until it has no soul in her eyes is surely just as bad isn't it?

The Greyhound Puppy Farm,

By Olga Ferguson, Scotland.

I had been volunteering for the local greyhound rescue for some time, when one evening the re-homing co-ordinator phoned me to say that she had had a disturbing phone call from a woman, claiming that in our city there was a stable, a former livery stables, where there were seventy greyhounds locked up and starving to death. The woman said that the man responsible had also stolen her horse. The rescue hoped that this was a hoax. However, there had also been an article in the local paper around the same time regarding the death of a horse at these stables. The man was being charged with cruelty by the *S.S.P.C.A.*, as the horse had somehow died of strangulation, whilst being loaded into a trailer. The newspaper article also mentioned that there were some sixty dogs at his premises. The article did not specify the breed, but as this place was not a registered boarding kennels, I knew that with that number of dogs there, something had to be very wrong. We read also that a decapitated greyhound pup had been found on the premises. The owner claimed that this had been done by someone else, in an act of vengeance against him. However, it was suspected by some that the owner himself had cut off the pup's head and gone to the newspapers with this fabricated story, to try to deflect the death of the horse away from himself.

Using a contact I had in another dog rescue, which was located just down the road from the stables, it was confirmed that there were indeed greyhounds being kept there in a neglected state. So, a party of volunteers went to the premises to investigate. There was no gate and the stables were not locked up. There was no one there, except, to the horror of the volunteers, in every stable they looked into, greyhounds were shut up in the darkness. Most of these were litters of pups of varying ages (ranging between three months and twelve months old) and the rest were brood bitches. Every stable was filthy; dog excrement everywhere, no food, no water and the dogs were starving and emaciated.

Several calls were made to the authority that deals with animal cruelty. Apparently, they had already visited the stables because of complaints by neighbouring house-holders, but they said that they were monitoring the situation and would not seize the dogs - yet.

Due to the critical state of some of the dogs, the rescue organised volunteers to give aid to the dogs. I visited the stables twice to help and this is what I saw.

This place was a hellhole. Next to the stable block was a muckheap, piled five metres high with excrement and dirty straw, a burnt out horse transporter and other rubbish. The stench was stomach turning and the pathetic, weak state of these animals was heartbreaking.

There were in total forty-four greyhounds, housed in approximately ten stables. All of the breeding bitches and the older pups were tattooed. Some of the bitches were on their own, whilst there was overcrowding in other sheds, where the litters had been kept together. Every dog, except one, was very underweight, full of worms, very cold as it was November, sick, with no water and some had infected sores. Dog faeces literally carpeted the floors of the sheds. The dogs also soiled in their pathetic, sodden blankets and bedding of wet straw and then lay in it, so dog faeces covered the puppies. These dogs were shut up in these cold, dark sheds twenty four hours a day, seven days a week.

The 'owner' of the dogs, a dangerous criminal, drug addict and drug dealer, had set up as a greyhound breeder some eighteen months prior to this horror being discovered. He had sent one young lad who used to stable his horse there to go and feed the dogs. But there was no dog food on the premises and this was an impossible task for one person. As they were starved, they fought over the food and each dog had to be separated to eat. There were no secure pens to put them in, so it required at least seven people to dish out the food, get the dogs onto slip leads, separate them and hold their leads whilst feeding. We also walked them around the adjacent field so that they could get out of their sheds for a short time. Then came the job of mucking out the sheds, hosing the floor down as best we could and providing fresh straw for bedding which had to be changed regularly. The older pups all crammed in together fought and tried to escape by jumping out of the top of the stable door if it was left open, so we had to bolt them in.

It was horrible having to return them to these sheds. Some refused to go back in and had to be carried. Most of these dogs had never been on a lead, or even seen the light of day, let alone been taken out of their sheds. Some were very distressed. One of these was a poor terrified, emaciated and scarred black male pup, of around nine months, whom we separated from his healthier looking brother. The two had been kennelled together and the fatter one (the only dog there that looked in reasonable shape) was aggressive and constantly attacking the other, eating all of what little food they ever got. That poor dog had a life of constant hell; not only cold, starving, lonely and terrified but attacked by another dog on a daily basis too. This poor boy was one of the first to be got out and went to a foster home, where he lasted less than twenty four hours, as so traumatised was he, that the fosterer could not cope. He then went onto another fosterer where he stayed several months. Because he was so nervous it took a long time to find him a forever home.

The brood bitches were in a terrible state. One beautiful, gentle, brindle bitch weighed about half of what she should have. Another fawn bitch, also kennelled alone, had clawed and chewed a large hole in the stable door so that she could have a small porthole to the outside world. Another fawn bitch was very weak and had large, open and infected sores on her legs. These bitches were Irish bred and had been transported over here as breeding machines.

As it appeared that the authorities were not going to act, the rescue started negotiations with the owner. At one point he warned us off going down there to feed the dogs. This was a very difficult situation that went on for a few weeks. As he was a violent thug, the rescue had to tread carefully.

The rescue decided that the only course of action to get the dogs out was to offer to purchase them from this man. This was something that I personally disagreed with, as I hoped that with further pressure, the authorities would take action, seize the dogs and prosecute him, but because people were now feeding and caring for them, it seemed that they could not do this.

Little by little, the dogs were bought, on average for £50 to £100 per dog, and rescued from the stables. Most went straight into foster homes, some to other rescues and some to the rescue's own kennels. After several weeks, all the dogs were gone from that place.

All these greyhounds eventually found loving new homes, but no case was ever brought against the breeder. Some were very traumatised and it was difficult to place them in homes. In many cases, the original fosterers adopted the pups. Most of the pups did not ever attain the stature of a normal greyhound, due to their poor start in life. I would recognise one of these stable pups anywhere, as they all had a very similar 'in-bred' look to them. Despite being tattooed for registration with the racing authorities, as one of the other volunteers put it "These dogs were bred for money, not for sport".

Saving Grace,

By Diane Bostock, England

In August my friend, Marie Keogh, phoned me to tell me of an elderly greyhound bitch who was in a rescue centre in Liverpool. She was in a bad way, very emaciated, with a large open tumour on her front leg. She was also suffering from arthritis. The centre was looking to find her a home as soon as possible. Sadly, there aren't many people who will take on dogs like these, but we were happy to have her.

Fate had it that Marie's husband, Cy, was working in Liverpool at the time, so late one Tuesday evening, at the end of August, she arrived with them both. Although I have seen many sad cases over the years, I was still shocked and saddened at the state this dear old lady was in. At the same time I was relieved to see that there was life in the old girl. I had feared that she was coming here to spend her final few weeks, or if she/we were lucky, her last few months.

I was instantly taken in with her beautiful face and even after all she must have been through during her life, she still wagged her tail to greet us. The greyhounds are such wonderful dogs and it is heartbreaking to think that the vast majority of them have to endure so much, knowing very little or nothing of comfort or kindness in their entire lives.

Grace had been picked up by the police who, because of the open tumour on her leg, thought she had been involved in a road traffic accident. They took her to one of the vets used by the rescue centre that Grace ended up in. Though the vets were unable to do anything about the tumour at the time, as Grace's condition was too poor, she was de-flead, vaccinated, wormed, microchipped and given Metacam for pain relief, before going onto *Freshfields* rescue centre.

Grace, who is a tall girl, only weighed 20kg when she was picked up but the worst thing was the tumour. She had literally licked all the skin off it, probably through boredom, as she was totally neglected by her owner. All the fur on her pressure points was worn down to the skin, so she must have been very uncomfortable. After she came to ours, I took her to our vet, Hywel, not very optimistically I must admit, to see if anything could be done as the tumour was in a place where there was very little spare skin. I came out feeling elated as Hywel felt confident that it could be removed. In his words, "it couldn't be left like that anyway." He said to give Grace another two to three weeks, to try to get a bit of weight on her before the operation. She had her operation on 21st September and it went very well, even though the main vein that runs down that leg went straight through the tumour. The lump was sent off for analysis and although the tumour will probably return, they are usually slow growing. Two weeks later, the stitches were removed and Hywel was very pleased with how it was looking. It had been a tricky operation with no guarantee of success. I was very pleased too that Hywel had done such an excellent job and given Grace a new lease of life.

Grace lives in the main part of the house and she loves lying on our comfy settees or in the giant beds with bedding four duvets thick! She also loves all the outdoor freedom that she gets here and thoroughly enjoys racing up and down the fencing with her new friends, sending off the cattle should they dare to come too close! Though Grace eats three meals a day, plus goodies, building her up is a slow process, as she was so wasted. Daily walks and having fun with the others are helping to build up her thigh muscles and she is starting to look better. We will, as we do with all of the dogs, do our utmost to make up for her eleven years of neglect and hardship.

I feel that several parties were instrumental in "saving" Grace; from the police to Withy Grove vets, to Freshfields and Marie and Cy who bought her here, enabling her to enjoy whatever time she has left. I know that could she talk, she would dearly like to each and everyone of them.

Scooby's Story,

By Donna Lynes, England

Scooby, formerly "James", illustrates how awful some humans can be towards a dog. Scooby was rescued, near to death, from an Irish dog fight gang, by *Ash Animal Rescue of Cork.*

The gang had tied him to a tree by his front legs, stabbed him to draw blood, cauterised the wound with the same knife, bloodied him (i.e. covered his back end with the blood) and then set the fighting dogs on him to make him fear for his life. This is how they train dogs for the ring. They use greyhounds because they have very little fur so the men can see their wounds and place bets before the greyhound dies. Scooby was only twelve months old when this happened.

He had been used as bait for the fighting and after his rescue, he was in danger of being kidnapped back by the gang. He is now recovering in our home in Somerset. He has suffered three emergency operations, one hundred and sixty four stitches and a sepsis infection of his blood.

Scooby is now one hundred percent recovered, assisted by Holly, the lurcher, and Josh, the Labrador cross. He is also under Angela Stockdale's expert guidance to re-socialize him. Scooby is a darling. He adores humans and he gives love, twenty four seven. He is ninety - percent greyhound, the rest is pure angel. He can often be found in he middle of Yeovil town helping me fund raise for greyhound rescue.

Scotts Kelly,

By Anthony Nevett, England

I own a retired greyhound called Scotts Kelly, who is seven years old. We have now had him for two years. After eighteen months I went on a Pets As Therapy course with him and now he visits stroke patients. He is a wonderful dog; a character and one of the family. He is so loving and loves his fuss. The patients look forward to him visiting and it is a pleasure when he brings smiles to their faces.

I got him from the *Retired Greyhound Trust*, in Addington, Northamptonshire. He looked at me and I just fell in love with those big brown eyes.

Sheri's Story,

By Lin, England

Sheri joined us when she was she was just over six years old. She had come into a rescue centre that I helped at. Her racing days were over and her owner had no more use for her. She wasn't used to people, but loved other dogs, especially greyhounds. We shared her life for just over two years, but she remained nervous and timid of all people, apart from us, who she trusted and was happy with.

Sheri had spent a year with us when we were made aware of another ex-racing greyhound that needed a home. Knowing that Sheri loved other greyhounds, we brought 'Poppy' home. It was love at first sight; Sheri adored Poppy, and her confidence doubled. At last she had a friend to relate to, and following a year of unsuccessfully trying to get Sheri to climb our stairs so that she could sleep with us, as soon as Poppy joined us on her first night, Sheri did too.

It was simply wonderful to see how happy Sheri was, and how inseparable she was from Poppy. However, we noticed that she had started to limp very slightly, and so we took her to the vet's. They weren't sure what was causing it, so suggested an x-ray. It was shockingly sad news, as there before our eyes we could see a tumour at the bottom of her leg, and she was given two to four weeks to live.

We were not about to give up on her, and we tried every alternative medication that we could. These treatments held back the cancer so successfully that a homeopathy vet thought that the tumour could be benign, because he thought she would have died before then if it really was cancer.

However, Sheri grew worse, walking and running on three legs almost all of the time. We decided to have her leg amputated. It was the only other choice that we had to try to give her life. Sheri had her whole leg and shoulder removed, hoping that any remaining cancer cells would not be left. She recovered, and was beginning to run and play with

Poppy on three legs, as she had done before her amputation, but after six weeks the tumour began to grow from almost where her shoulder was. Within another two weeks the tumour had grown to the size of an orange, and we could no longer control her pain. We could do no more.

I went to the vet's to collect a sedative for her, and by the time our vet came to our home, Sheri never even felt the needle. For just over two years this big, beautiful, harmless, gentle, Irish girl was treasured and loved so very much. Our pain in losing her was knowing that her life should have been for longer. Our gorgeous girl is loved and missed every day.

Silly Tilly,

By SandraBigley

Everyday the *Manchester Evening News* runs a photo and a brief appeal about a dog. On Saturday, 16th April, 2005, I was feeling guilty because I knew my old greyhound was preparing to go to heaven and I wanted her approval of any successor. Somehow it had never happened that I had got one. Experience having taught me the power of prayer, I prayed earnestly that my apparent failure might be turned to good account and that I was being saved for someone special. Tilly's photograph was in that night's edition of the *M.E.N* but I was sure she was not really available for re-homing. She was advertised as an old greyhound (at six!) in need of a caring home. She was unable to be re-homed with small animals or small children and was a loving old dog who would be a happy with an older person who could give her all the love and cuddles she needs.

Sure enough, when I phoned the next day I was told that she was in the sick bay and not able to be re-homed. I made a fuss. "O.k," they said, "you can come and look at her but she is too ill to be re-homed."

Assuring my husband that I was only going to look, I packed the home team in the car (two cavaliers and a greyhound), packed the latest photos of the previous dog I had removed by devious means, Nikkie, and went to *Manchester Dogs'* Home. Eerily it was again their Spring Opening Day, the same day that I had got Nikkie out two years before.

When I arrived they said, "You can't see her. She is in the sick bay." "But I have come all this way especially," I said in an artless dismay, "and you promised on the telephone that you would let me see her." "O.k" they said, "but you cannot take her. She is too poorly."
Well, this miserable scrap could not stop weeing in stress and her legs were decidedly wobbly. She was visibly covered in scurf, cuts, bald patches and fleas. We tested her with the other dogs, including my greyhound, Luka. I produced the pictures of Nikkie and before I knew it they were offering to give her to me NOW. "But, but," I protested, "I

promised my husband I was only looking and I have not got a suitable crate."

"We'll help you," they said as they bundled us all into the car.

"I bet you won't help explain to my husband!" I responded. The amazing thing is that Tilly even has a certificate which says she was "not suitable for rehoming."

When I got home I left the others in the car and walked through to greet my husband, who did not initially realise that the greyhound on the lead was not our own dear Luke but a newcomer. We rallied around as you do and found a hound-sized crate to borrow, not that Tilly needed it for behavioural reasons. She practically sobbed in relief to be back in a proper home again. Once greyhounds have known a domestic home they cannot cope with kennels again.

The next morning she was checked over by my vet. She appeared to have had two recent sets of dental work done, of poor quality. We did not initially realise why. She not only had dirty ears, fleas and scurf but also something I had never heard of, called fur mites. These are highly contagious but had not been diagnosed before, or they definitely would not have released her to me. In fact if they had been diagnosed it seems likely that she would have been put to sleep immediately, as they are hard to treat, but more of that later. I spent the rest of Monday washing everything she had come into contact with.

She had lost the end of her tail, probably through excessive wagging, as she proved to be the cheeriest dog. She had nasty cuts on her forepaws that were initially expected to heal quickly. She also had a racing/lamping injury to one of her back paws. Both her front knee joints were swollen with arthritis. I thought that was all!

After a couple of weeks I noticed her breath was becoming bad, very bad. This proved to be trench mouth. This is an incurable condition that is rumoured to develop from a combination of stress and malnutrition, in British troops at least. Mercifully, this too was not diagnosed at the Dogs' Home, as that would have been a death warrant.

Once she had settled, we found that she was the cheekiest, waggiest dog, already neutered. She gave me a great surprised me one day. As I was doing the daily training session with my other dogs, she came up behind me, poked me, and demonstrated that she could do tricks too.

I had tried to trace her ear tattoos. Right ear tattoos normally means that the dog is an English racer, and both ears normally means Irish. Wrong, in this case!!! When I phoned Ireland they were adamant that her ear tattoos were not recognised by them, so that meant she had to be a flap-tracker.

Dogs are totally honest so this is my educated guess at her history, based on what we do know about her. She was born and brought up in someone's kitchen, a domestic environment certainly, perhaps with a flap-tracking family. She became the pet/trainee racer of the son of the family. She was neutered. She was beaten if she tried to go upstairs. The family had other dogs that barked. He was a teenage lad who grew into a stocky young man. He spent time with her, teaching her new tricks and he raced her. He grew up and left home. She grew too old for racing and now she was useless the lad was told not to worry. He was told she would be given to someone who would look after her. She was probably used for lamping a bit. Then she got the injured foot. Her front paws were tied together and she was literally thrown to the dogs. How she managed to survive is anybody's guess but she must have suffered a period of starvation and stress to give her the trench mouth.

So, now after nine months with us she is very happy. She adores her little fluffy friends, the cavaliers, and is becoming increasingly protective of them. She is fine with children too, so the advert, saying she was no good with children or small animals, was completely wrong.

She has her teeth washed in salt water, two to three times a day and all her food has to be softened. She can't manage hard biscuits and I suspect that, even though I am winning in the battle against the trench mouth, I am losing the battle against the plaque. Her swollen arthritic knee joints and broken toe are still bathed daily in salt water, as are her forepaw cuts. They appear to be healing, but only just. She is also given cider vinegar every day. One of the knees has healed but the other is still swollen. The bare patches have gone and the stump of her tail has grown over. There are no fleas, fur mites or scurf, following the six highly toxic baths. At the time, little did I realise the stress I was putting her under by carrying her upstairs for these baths, because of her previous beatings.

She still cannot run. According to a passing Chinese osteopathic acupuncturist (you meet all sorts down by the river!) her muscles still "remember" those beatings so we will see what the future brings. For those of you who have read this far, you may wonder what happened to Luka. Well, I had been carrying her up to bed for months. One night she could not walk the rest of the way. At about three a.m. she leant across the bed to Tilly and did that deep sort of handing over sniff that they do. She died the next day.

By the grace of God, I saved Tilly from an early, undeserved euthanasia. She saved me from mourning my beloved Luka.

Snowy's Story,

By Geoff Richardson, England

Snowy's story begins in a litter-strewn lay-by at the side of a main road leading into a large city in the North of England. A few days previously my partner, Marilyn, and I had received a visit from Karen and her husband Dennis, who run an extremely busy greyhound rescue charity. They came on a mission; would we be prepared to foster an elderly greyhound bitch that desperately needed re-homing, called Snowy? At the time we had only one rescued greyhound, Frank, living with us so we could not refuse.

So, on a bright, clear spring afternoon, I came to be sitting in a lay-by waiting for a car to pull in behind me and subsequently to follow me to our home. I had not been waiting long when a car arrived. I walked round to say hello to Snowy, her owner, who was driving and a young man who later proved to be the owner's brother. But, I couldn't see Snowy. There was no visible evidence of a greyhound and her owner was decidedly cool in her attitude towards me. She seemed agitated and wanted to hurry so I was soon pulling out of the lay-by onto the very busy dual carriageway. In doing so I automatically looked into my rear view mirror and was surprised to see the young man leaning over the back of his seat flailing his arms about; did I see him hitting something, was that a thump? Or were my eyes deceiving me? After all I was driving in heavy traffic and my concentration was already fully occupied.

We soon arrived outside our home and I walked round to the other car. Snowy's owner was already out and opening the rear door. There was Snowy, crouched down behind the front seat, laying flat to the floor. She clearly knew her place in life, literally! She was obviously cowering.

I was almost in a state of shock; I just couldn't believe that just a few minutes previously I had witnessed, all be it by chance, a grown man battering an elderly greyhound into submission. I had to get her away from them quickly but it wasn't that easy.

Snowy's owner, obviously wishing to impress me with her concern for the welfare of this cream-coloured greyhound, insisted that Marilyn and I brought Frank out to meet Snowy, to ensure that they would get on together. This matter was quickly resolved, there being no problems with the introduction of the two dogs, and soon we were all indoors having a cup of tea. Snowy's owner, presenting us with a soiled piece of blanket and a tin of dog food, dabbed her eyes with a tissue and commenced to inform us just how much she was suffering at the thought of parting with Snowy.

Meanwhile, I noticed that after a few minutes "greyhound chat" with Frank, Snowy seemed to be trying to make herself invisible by hiding behind the television. I became aware of a rather nasty odour had permeated the room. When it became obvious that we had all detected this smell, Snowy's owner remarked that it was unwise to allow Snowy to lick your face as she had a dirty mouth.

Then they were gone. At last Snowy's suffering at their hands had ended. I breathed a big sigh of relief and picked up the telephone. Two hours later, Snowy was being examined by a rather shocked and disgusted veterinary surgeon. Poor Snowy; the infection in her mouth had been allowed to develop to such an extent that it was now life threatening and without surgery she had days left to live. Just what agony she had silently suffered I can't imagine. Arrangements were made for Snowy to have the necessary surgery and with a course of antibiotics in hand, I returned home. I rang the rescue service, only to discover that Snowy's previous owner had, in fact, just recently received a substantial grant from the rescue service to finance the treatment that she so badly needed! This money was certainly was not spent at the vet's.

Within a few weeks of the surgery, Snowy's health had improved so much that other people did not realise that she was the same dog that had arrived in such a state of ill health. Her remaining few teeth were gleaming white, her coat now had a silky sheen, her eyes were bright and incredibly warm and as her health began to improve, I noticed her taking stock of her surroundings. She examined, sniffed or even licked everything that she could reach.

She noted the position of every article both in the house and in the rear garden and was aware if anything had been moved, even slightly. However, in Snowy's eyes, the first major job was to make sure that Frank was well cared for and didn't he just love it! She insisted that she washed his face at least once a day and within a few weeks, they would often curl up together on one of their beds. On one occasion, we were watching television and Frank was laid in front of the fire. Snowy, presumably wanting a drink, decided to go through to the kitchen, which meant she had to pass by Frank. She attracted my attention when, on reaching the door, she came to an abrupt halt. There was obviously something on her mind. Snowy then did a sharp about turn, walked back to Frank and proceeded to give his face a thorough wash. That was typical of Snowy, who is nothing if not conscientious.

During this initial settling in period, Snowy's actions illustrated just what kind of life she had led previously. For instance, it took many nights of soft persuasion to get her to accept the fact that she was allowed to lay in front of the fire. It was especially noticeable at bedtime that she instinctively headed for the door. Obviously, she had been used to being put out at night; we believe that she had been sleeping on concrete. Evidence of this was to be found in the various calloused, bald spots around her frame.

However, Snowy did recover; she did begin to realise that she was allowed to enjoy life and this was to be confirmed by a particular incident whilst we were on holiday in North Wales. It was a glorious summer's day and we were on a vast expanse of beach. The tide was well out, the sea just barely visible on the horizon. Both Snowy and Frank were off their leads and just tinkering about in the odd rock pool when suddenly Snowy took us all by surprise. She ran off! She kept running until she was just a spot in the distance. Had her life been that bad that she still felt she needed to escape from even us? Frank was clearly perplexed; he couldn't make out what was happening and just stood at my side. My heart was in my mouth.

Then she stopped and looked back at us. She began to run again but this time not away from us but in a massive circle and we were standing at its centre.

She ran like the wind. Rocks were to be leapt over and pools to be splashed through. She jumped and darted from side to side. Somehow I knew that she was casting off all the agonies, humiliations and pain that this ten year old greyhound had thought were normal and acceptable. She was experiencing something quite new in her life; she was happy. No, not just happy, it was more than that. It was possibly the first time in her life that she was truly glad to be alive. And she knew it!

Snowy changed that day. She decided that not only was she responsible for Frank's welfare but also Marilyn's and mine. She adopted what can only be described as a maternal attitude towards us all. This didn't just involve her attempts to make sure that we all stayed clean, with regular washes, but she immediately ran in front if she sensed danger. The very best she could offer was a deep growl; she completely disregarded the fact that her gums were virtually toothless!

She also would show her disapproval at certain events as well. She much preferred things to stay as they were. As I mentioned previously, she had taken stock of almost everything in the house and garden and she was well aware if anything had been moved. This would provoke a low vocal grumbling of disapproval but that was all. Snowy never displayed anything that could be described as anger.

Snowy wasn't with us for long, less than two years. One Saturday morning at four a.m. we were awoke by the sound of her crying in agony. Such were her cries that it was obvious that something was very seriously wrong. We got out our sleeping bags and spent the rest of the night on the living room floor with her. Two aspirins seemed to give Snowy some relief from the torment that she was clearly going through. At 8:15 a.m. she was standing on the vet's table. The situation was irretrievable. It is not necessary to say anymore, except, the vet's opinion was that an old racing injury had probably caught up with her.

However, I can't help suspecting that the raining down of several well aimed thumps in the car, by the brother of her previous owner, could well have been the cause of undetected, long-term damage. Yes, I wonder, did I handle that situation correctly? Or do I still feel so angry that it distorts my views on the matter?

Snowy was missed by all of us and Frank insisted on searching every room in the house every day for the first two to three weeks after we lost her. At times he would look at me in the way that greyhounds do, a kind of a questioning look over the top of his proud nose; that kind of uncanny, non-verbal communication that greyhounds are capable of. We knew that he was missing Snowy, in fact he did at times cold-shoulder me for a while as I was the one who took her out and didn't bring her home.

There is a little more to add to Snowy's short story. When I rang Karen to let her know that we had lost her she mentioned that, when Snowy had first come to live with us, she had received a phone call from her previous owner saying that Snowy wouldn't ever fit in with us, as she was a problem dog and she simply refused to be house trained. Snowy, apparently, had terrible habits and we wouldn't put up with her. After all the mental and physical abuse that had been bestowed upon Snowy, her previous owner still felt it necessary to assassinate her character. Why? Could it be that she was worried that Snowy would, as always, communicate the truth to us, in her own way? Was she frightened of Snowy? Did she fear that Snowy's loving and honest innocence would prove more powerful than a human's superior physical strength and mental abilities? That, in the most important way of all, the truth would out?

What do you think?

Tally,

By Mary Musette Stewart, America

John and I had been together for several years and had many heated discussions over whether or not we were ready to adopt a dog. I already had two cats and John's dog preference did not excite me very much. You see John wanted a greyhound. I just could not understand what he thought was so wonderful about having a greyhound. I mean, to me they seemed too skinny, they did not seem to be playful, they never seem happy, and they do not get along well with kitty cats. So what was so great about having a greyhound? Well, as I have since discovered, everything!

Even though I did not want a greyhound, I did want to have a happy husband. And unfortunately for him, John had been going through a rough time at work and there was very little that was causing him much happiness. So after a lot of discussions with my vet over whether or not a greyhound would cause harm to my kitty cats, and after much research on the breed, I decided I would adopt a greyhound as a surprise to John. How hard could it be to pick one out, I thought. Little did I know the problem would not be finding one that I liked, but finding one that I did not like, because as I soon discovered, I liked them all! This is why I ended up having to disclose my surprise to John before I had actually picked one out.

I will never forget the evening I set out on finding the right greyhound. I had met someone from *Greyhound Ranch* Adoptions, at a meet and greet and I was told that the Ranch was literally a short distance from my house. So, on a Friday night, after work, I went to the Ranch to see what my options were. I did not really have a preference over whether I wanted a male or a female, or what color, or anything like that. All I knew is that I wanted a friendly, fun-loving greyhound that was cat friendly. So Leslie, the Ranch owner, set out to help me find the right greyhound. She must have brought out fifteen dogs for me to meet that evening. I was so surprised to discover that every one of them seemed happy and definitely liked to play. When Leslie would let one out of it's crate, he or she would run down the ramp and do circles in the yard and eventually make its way over to where I was standing to meet me. In essence, all of them had to do a little showing off and stretching of the legs before deciding that it was a good idea to approach the woman watching them in awe. That is, all except Saint.

Saint was different from the others and I liked him right away. When Leslie let Saint out of his crate, he came strolling down the ramp, looked to the right, then looked to the left, which is where I was sitting at this point, and then walked right over to me and never left my side. He was content to just look me in the eye and accept the kisses I was giving him. Boy was I excited! I thought I had found the perfect greyhound. But Leslie was not so sure. She said Saint had not been cat tested and there was no way of truly knowing how he would be around cats until he had been cat tested. But I am an optimist and I just knew everything would work out. And it did, but unfortunately, not with Saint.

I was so excited about adopting Saint that I broke the surprise and told John what I had been up to. I told him he just had to meet Saint. So, on that Sunday, he and I went to the Ranch together and he met Saint. And Saint was definitely drawn to both of us. There was another couple at the Ranch, at the time, that were looking for a male greyhound, and they liked Saint. But each time they petted Saint he would indulge them for a minute and come right back over to John and I. It was as if he knew he was going home with us. Later that evening, however, John told me that he decided that he did not want to get a dog. He had listened to all of my concerns about how greyhounds can be harmful to cats. He felt a dog was too much responsibility, and he had decided he just did not want one. You would have thought I would have been happy since I did not want a dog to begin with, but I wasn't. On the contrary, I was devastated. So devastated in fact that I did not even sleep well that night but I did come up with a plan. When I got to work on Monday morning I wrote a "Top 25 List of Reasons Why We Should Adopt Saint", and I came up with four reasons why we shouldn't. But of the four reasons why we shouldn't, all of them could be worked out. Of course I ended my "Top 25 List" by telling John that I loved Saint and

I would never forgive him if he did not let me have him. So, he gave in and said ok.

After work that evening, I drove straight to the Ranch and filled out the adoption paperwork. As it turns out, Leslie could not get a vet appointment any time soon and then she was going out of town for a week so I had to wait to bring Saint home. It almost drove me crazy. But every day, after work, I would drive to the Ranch and visit Saint. We would play and I would give him kisses and tell him how happy I was that I was bringing him home. Meanwhile, Leslie's concerns about him not being cat friendly grew. She had been watching him closely and noticed how he was very interested in the turtle in her yard and in the things going on outside her yard. On one occasion, his interest grew so great that he actually ran smack into her fence while trying to go after some people riding behind the Ranch on dirt bikes. I was still optimistic but I did mention Leslie's concerns to John and I told him I still wanted a greyhound even if we could not have Saint. I wanted to know if there was another greyhound that he had met and liked. His response to me was that he thought they were all nice and it did not matter to him which one we got.

On a Friday evening three weeks after meeting Saint, I decided to help Leslie at a meet-and greet at a local elementary school. We had fifteen dogs with us and Saint was one of them. Interestingly enough, unlike how he normally acted, Saint completely ignored me! Instead, two females, Tally and Fury, did everything but actually jump up in my lap! Even though I had met Fury before and I really liked her, I was drawn to Tally. Tally was supposed to be adopted by someone else but that person decided she wanted to adopt a Doberman instead. So, Tally was once again up for adoption.

Tally is a petite red fawn with the most soulful eyes I have ever seen on an animal. Part of her attractiveness to me may have come from the fact that she also had scars on her back from where the person who tried to breed her let the male dogs bite her, to the point that her scars are so deep they will never go away. Tally was not a very fast runner so her racing career was short lived so the owner then tried to breed her. Leslie got Tally and another female dog because their owner's wife called Leslie and said her husband had put so many dogs down lately that she could not take it anymore. She told Leslie she had two days to pick up the two females or they would be killed. I felt so bad for Tally ; all I wanted to do was take care of her, make it all better, and make her forget about the past mistreatment and abuse she suffered.

The next day I decided I wanted to bring Tally to my house to see how she reacted to my kitty cats. Unfortunately the weather was not cooperating and it did not seem like a good idea to bring her over that day. But on the following day, I called Leslie and told her what I had in mind. She said it would be no problem at all. So I picked up Tally and we rode home. Once we got there the first thing I did was introduce her to my cats. When Tally saw them, she actually turned her head away and would not even look at them. It was like she was saying, "I don't know what those things are, but I don't want any part of them!" Her reaction was actually very wonderful because I knew I would not have to worry about her being too interested in the cats and causing them any harm.

We then went into the living room and I put a blanket down on the floor for Tally and I told her to lay down. She looked at me like she had no idea what I was talking about and it occurred to me that she might not know what I meant. So I laid down and encouraged her to lay down next to me. What she did next completely sealed the deal. She actually laid down, put her head on my arm, and moved right up against me, to get as close to me as she could. I couldn't believe it. I knew then and there that she was the absolutely perfect dog for me and I could not wait to tell my husband.

When John got home from playing golf, Tally was still over and so I introduced him to our new greyhound. Of course, he loved her immediately. When I took her back to the Ranch, I told Leslie that I really liked Tally and wanted to adopt her but I was still extremely fond of Saint. Leslie told me she was very concerned about Saint and felt that Tally would be the better choice, especially since she had such a good reaction to the kitty cats. And as it turns out, when Leslie took

Saint to the vet a couple of days later she discovered that Saint was definitely not cat friendly. So it worked out perfectly.

That Friday, Leslie brought Tally over for good and my life has never been the same since. I have discovered that there is no dog better than a greyhound and I will have a greyhound in my life until the day I die. I will also do all that I can to find homes for other greyhounds and stop the abuse that the greyhounds sometimes suffer. Even though my husband does not want another one, I have discovered that one is just not enough. My love for Tally is so deep that I want her to be as happy as she can be and I want to get her a greyhound playmate. And hopefully one day I will! But until then, I am so thankful that I have Tally. I thank my husband practically every day for wanting a greyhound and for opening my eyes to the wonderful breed. And I think the bumper sticker I bought for the back of my car sums it up perfectly, "My heart belongs to my greyhound." It always will.

The Irish Two,

By Amanda Wells, Scotland

I booked a cottage on the County Galway coast, on a remote island, for a week, for my children and I. Initially we were going to take our dogs, but I have not spent much quality time with the children over the last few months because it has been so hectic, changing jobs and campaigning, that my parents suggested keeping the dogs and letting us go alone.

About two weeks before we went, Bernie from *Dog Rescue Ireland* in Dublin, forwarded an email from a racing greyhound owner in Belfast, asking her to take his greyhound because the dog kept injuring himself on the track so it was not 'economic sense' to keep him. He said that although he really didn't want to have the dog destroyed, he would have to, unless she took him. Bernie, in her usual position, is jam packed full of these 'disposable dogs' so wasn't in a position to take him on. I was going via Belfast so offered to pick the dog up if anyone else could take him and Dave Linford of *Poplar Farm Kennels* in Peterborough offered the grey a kennel space. We made the final arrangements and I called Belfast several times to speak with the owner, who was never in, but I confirmed that I would pick the dog, Tullyglen Buoy, up from him and his son. Several other people were involved in communicating with the owner and his family throughout this stage.

A few days before we left for Galway, we arranged a 'relay' of individuals to transport the greyhound south to Dave. It was arranged that we would arrive home on the Saturday night and travel down to Peterborough on the Sunday morning.

Through the week Dave called me a few times. Firstly, he had come across a greyhound bitch that was due to be destroyed through a woman he knew in the North. I agreed to bring the bitch back with me too. He then got a plea for help from Bernie. A man had called her and told her that he was going to prison on the Thursday and if she didn't take his greyhound, he would cut its ears off and abandon it. Bernie was understandably quite upset. However, as we knew we had to get the greyhound away from his owner and it's always risky to put two male greyhounds together, we had to turn her down. Bernie managed to fit in the other male to her already overcrowded place, although Bernie finds it quite difficult to re-home greyhounds in Ireland as they simply are not seen as pets.

On my return from Galway to the North, I received a phone call from the wife of the owner of the greyhound we were to pick up. She told us that she had our lunch ready and that she would meet us at the bottom of the road so she could take us to her house. I stammered; no way did I want to sit at a table with any one involved in this 'sport'. However, we met as planned and were taken to a house. The couple were very friendly and talkative. If I put my beliefs aside I could have even liked them. I was taken to the back of the house where there was a concrete 'pen' with an eight-foot fence. It was about six feet by twelve. At the back were three garden huts, obviously where the greyhounds lived. Three dogs were stretched up at the fence barking and wagging their tails. The stench coming from them was pretty awful. All three dogs were dirty but seemed happy enough.

The man spoke all the time to me about how fast the dogs raced and how good his dogs were. He also told me that Tullyglen Buoy was good but he didn't take the bends at the track very well and often came away injured. He said he was a 'dud one' and that he wouldn't ever dream of putting him to sleep, but knew his racing days were over. I kept my mouth closed thinking that I'd seen the email of what his intent was. He took me into his house and showed me all the trophies his dogs had won. He had framed photos of his dogs winning races all over the place. Particular pride of place went to photos of a dog that had won the Ulster Cup. He kept telling me what a good racer Tullyglen was and how he could win a race tonight if he wanted. His children and baby granddaughter were there, as was the family Jack Russell who was extremely overweight and very spoiled.

I spoke to the wife and she admitted to me that often you hear people at the track saying that their dog is retiring. You apparently never see the dog again and never ask where its gone because you know its either been killed and buried or taken to the vet. They spoke about one of their greyhounds that had bone cancer. This brought me to ask about the bone cancer that is predominant in some breeding lines of greyhounds. They told me that everyone knows that this was because the dog that many greyhounds are bred from was injected full of 'dope'. I asked them if they were sure of this and they said 'Oh yes, everyone knows that!' They told me that the descendants of this dog get bone cancer at very young ages and mostly are put to sleep before it progresses. They also believe that we don't know the scale of the problem because the dogs are destroyed and there are no questions asked.

One of the daughters had been speaking to my children and asked me if it was true that I kept three greyhounds as pets and that they slept in my bed. I said, "Yes." She looked at me like I had just admitted to eating my goldfish. The couple went on to admit that they were breeding from an eight-year-old bitch. Its unclear whether she is Tullyglen's mother, but they did proudly tell me that Tullyglen was bred and born on the 4th May 2000 in that very back yard. They also admitted that Tullyglen was being replaced almost immediately. Tullyglen's sister was nowhere to be seen but they did admit that up until a few weeks ago there were six dogs there. I have no idea where any of the others went.

The man produced four stamped vaccination cards and told me to pick one because they were all the same. The only part of the card that was completed was the details of vaccinations received. Even the breed part was blank. The owner told me that Tullyglen had been wormed and had 'Frontline' flea treatment the week before. They told me Tullyglen's pet name was 'Whitey'. He didn't respond to that name at all. We have since settled on Tully as he suits that better. As we were leaving the woman pushed £20 into my hand. The man helped me get Tully into the boot (I have a hatchback!). As he shut the boot, I noticed his expression change as he saw the sticker; 'A Greyhound Is For Life – Not Just For Racing'.

Meanwhile the woman from the shelter in the North called me. I was way behind time and it was agreed that a man would drive down to the ferry terminal and meet me there. I met the man and he looked relieved to see me. He opened the back door of the van and I caught sight of probably the prettiest greyhound I have ever seen. She was small, white and fawn and had an air about her. She was gorgeous! We were passed our check-in time by now so I only had a few minutes to get all I could from the man about her. She didn't have a collar, just a rope lead. They had just had her neutered and vaccinated and he gave me her details and paperwork. She didn't have a name and she wasn't good getting into cars. She had been picked up as a stray and taken to the pound.

Because there is no hope of getting a home for a greyhound in Ireland, most greyhounds are put to sleep immediately. A woman at the shelter and another woman, who I will leave nameless, but will never be able to thank enough, managed to have her registered as a 'lurcher.' Her death warrant, by revealing her true breed, was never signed. However, she is a true greyhound and more than likely was a racer, as her ears have tattoos. I worked out that the tattoo mark made her two years old. Before the man left, he asked me to please find a way of helping the greyhounds there. He said if I could find homes for them in Scotland they would even get the ferry over to meet me at Stranraer. He said they were desperate for help otherwise they would just have to keep killing them. I promised him I would try to help him.

We drove into the ferry terminal. Tully was very unsettled; panting and really over-excited, so we stepped out of the car with them. Tully wouldn't drink water no matter how we tried. The bitch didn't seem to care about him. She paid no attention to anything really. The children decided we'd call her 'Claddagh'. We had been to the Claddagh part of Galway where the women traditionally wear the Claddagh Ring. This symbolises love, friendship and trust, which is what we hope for Claddagh' s future.

Unfortunately we had to leave the dogs downstairs as no dogs are allowed on deck on the fast ferry. We couldn't get the slow one because I get very sick on it. I worried the whole journey. When we did get back to the car, Tully was in an awful state. He was panting hard, howling and barking. Claddagh was curled up asleep. We stopped at Stranraer where I gave Tully the last of the water and gave him a little walk. He was so uptight and excited. His panting did not get any easier. We drove up to Girvan, where I bought another bottle of water. We then took both of them for a long walk on the beach. The beach amazed Claddagh; she kept stopping to look out to sea. It was like she'd never seen the sea before. I noticed she was also quite jumpy when she saw passing cars. I think she came from a rural place.

We stopped again but Tully didn't stop panting nor did he seem to calm down. We arrived home and got out the car. Tully cocked his leg and was urinating blood. I was so worried and called Dave. Dave said he didn't know what was up, but it sounded like something soldiers used to get after marching for too long. We decided that the best course of action was for me to call my vet. I phoned the emergency vet and told her what had happened. She advised me that this was actually not blood but muscle wastage passing through his kidneys. She said this is common in greyhounds when they get over excited and often happens when they overdo racing. She advised that I keep Tully as cool and calm as possible and make him drink lots to wash it through. She told me that if he were still the same the next morning to get him in to the vet's, as he would need to go on a drip. I told her that he was to travel south in the morning. She warned me strongly against this saying that he must not travel until at least Tuesday. It was settled; they were staying here until Tully got better.

The first night I shut them in my living room when I finally went to bed at 3 a.m. Tully howled and barked the whole night. Fortunately, I don't have neighbours so I was able just to leave him. I was very aware that what I did could affect his re-homing. In the morning he was urinating normally. However, I did notice that he was crawling with fleas and that he had worms.

On the Tuesday we took both to the vet. The vet was not happy with Tully's urine sample and advised he should be taken back on Friday before the second attempt at taking him to Peterborough. The vet agreed that his vaccination card was not only a year out of date but extremely dodgy and we agreed to have him vaccinated again. The vet believed this as there was no way Tully had been 'Frontlined" or wormed the week before. She asked me what Tully was being fed on. I told her the owner said he'd been fed things like chicken. The vet advised me to continue on the low protein food as him being over excited and boisterous could be down to his diet.

Claddagh was given a clean bill of health and had her stitches from being neutered removed. She is underweight but the vet believes that both dogs will be fine when they receive some tender loving care. Tully returned to the vet on Friday and although he has protein in his urine still, he was healthy enough to be neutered.

Since that first night, Tully has been fine at night and o.k. about being left. He is rather boisterous and very clumsy, but he is such a nice natured dog. Claddagh is so affectionate and stands for long periods of time being petted. Both dogs are finding things like the washing machine, stairs, the hoover, and cars, a little odd. However, both have now settled in well and have met my three other greyhounds and the cat. My cat hates dogs and has sorted them out; they've not attempted to chase her after she thumped them.

Both of them seem a lot happier. They are very attached to us already and so affectionate and trusting. I worry about Claddagh though as she is very quiet. If only they could talk and tell you what has happened in their short lives, but then I think it's just as well we don't know.

I have barely slept since I came home. I can't stop wishing that I'd taken a van and collected the dogs at the cottage in Galway and there has been several times where I have talked myself out of going back to get them. And if we did? The owners would just get themselves others. I have been thinking hard about what we can do for the Irish greyhounds. What can we do? Save a few? Help ease the burden from the likes of Bernie of Greyhound Action, Ireland, and others who do all they can? There is something seriously wrong. My sensible head and my friends and family tell me that I can't save them all. However, my heart says I must try and help the dogs. People tell me the campaign is more important because we need to stop the cause rather than just try and block the leaking tap of greyhounds. I know this and feel stronger about things than I ever have before.

The saddest thing is that there will be fifteen thousand Tully's and Claddagh's this year. This will be in Ireland alone. The bottom line is that we'll never even get to the tip of the iceberg. I look at my three and the Irish two and I think they are the lucky ones...

Postscript: I couldn't do it - both are staying in Scotland with me!

Trek and Ryhndda,

By Sue Cotton, England

This is a story about how we spent our millennium night. It revolves around Trek, the most handsome greyhound I have ever seen, and Rhyndda, a sleek, athletic black greyhound.

Trek was abandoned in Leamington Spa. He is an English bred dog with no traceable racing history, so he may have been used on the flapping tracks. He was five years old when we got him from a rescue centre, where he had lived for three years, unable to find a new home. Rhyndda was raced until she was seven years old. It is very unusual for a dog to be raced until that age. She must have been very good, but unfortunately her racing owner could not find it in his heart to repay her hard work and racing skills with a home in which to retire. She was sent to a re-homing centre. I chose her as a companion for Trek.

All we heard about as the new Millennium approached was how many fireworks everyone was having, and how loud and big they would be. All I could think about was the terror that lay ahead for our two dogs on that night. Like many dogs, they are terrified of thunder and fireworks. To make matters worse, my shiny black girl, Rhyndda, had an operation to remove her spleen a couple of days before bonfire night. As she lay trembling with fear, feeling so ill that night, I comforted her and told her that she would never have to feel that fear again. But what could we do?

We racked our brains, and my husband Dean came up with the solution. We would just go, take the dogs and go. The day before New Years Eve, we collected a people carrier from the hire garage. The next day, we loaded it up with picnics for the dogs and ourselves, dog beds, sleeping bags, water bowls and half a bottle of champagne. We set of for the wilderness of Wales.

We drove for about three hours and found a nice grassy area on the edge of the Radnor forest on top of a hill somewhere. We took Trek and

Rhyndda for a short walk by the light from the headlights, then settled down for our food and listened to the radio. At the stroke of midnight, we opened our bubbly and poured fresh water for the dogs. The whole sky around us lit up like a giant electric storm from those huge fireworks, but not a sound was heard by the dogs! We had a nap, then headed home with two beautifully calm greyhounds.

Everyone said it was like every bonfire night rolled into one. I am so glad we missed it!

I would like there to be a happy ending to the story, but on January 28th we lost our shiny black girl to the terrible cancer that took her away from us. I will always remember our millennium night; where I was, the special friends we shared it with and the promise I made to her and kept.

Greyhound Racing – The Awful Facts.

By Greyhound Action

Tens of thousands of dogs are disposed of every year by the British greyhound racing industry, because they fail to make the grade as racers or when their racing days are over.

About 30,000 greyhound pups are registered every year in the British Isles. The number bred is actually many thousands more than this, when taking into account pups that never get registered and those killed by breeders at a very young age.

Although most of these dogs are bred in Ireland, the majority are produced to supply the demands of the British greyhound racing industry. Thousands of greyhound pups and young dogs are put to death because they fail to reach racing standards. We estimate that over 10,000 are killed annually in the British Isles.

Dogs which actually make it to the track are very likely to experience suffering during their racing careers. It has been estimated that greyhounds running on British tracks sustain many thousands of injuries every year and that 10% of dogs that race are already suffering from injuries. Injured toes, torn muscles, strained tendons and arthritic joints are commonplace.

At least 12,000 greyhounds "retire" from racing in Britain every year, at an average age of just 2½ years old. This is either because of injury or because they are judged to be no longer good enough to race.
Very few of these dogs manage to find good homes. This is hardly surprising in a country where many thousands of ordinary "pet" dogs are put to sleep every year because no homes are available for them.

The British greyhound racing industry has admitted that 500 - 1,000 retired greyhounds are put to death every year. This alone would be enough to justify a ban on greyhound racing, but the true figure for retired dogs killed is, sadly, far, far higher. Quite possibly as many as 7,000. Many ex-racing greyhounds are simply abandoned and a large number are killed, sometimes by extremely cruel methods such as drowning or poisoning, because some owners and trainers are not prepared to pay the cost of having them put to sleep by a vet. We are receiving an increasing number of reports of trainers shooting dogs when their racing days are over.

We don't wish to suggest that everyone involved in greyhound racing is cruel or insensitive. There are some "owners" and trainers who love their dogs and take good care of them for the whole of their natural lives. But this only applies to a small minority of the thousands of dogs which enter racing.

Every year many hundreds of "unwanted" greyhounds are shipped to Spain to be kept for racing in appalling conditions or used for hunting and coursing. Dogs which turn out to he no good for hunting are often brutally disposed of, with hanging being a favourite method.

The only way to prevent the massive suffering and killing of greyhounds, caused by the greyhound racing industry, is for greyhound racing to be abolished. It is interesting to note that this has already happened in the USA, where six states have banned greyhound racing since 1993. In the meantime it is important that people avoid attending or betting on greyhound racing, so that it gradually comes to an end through lack of finance and support.

GREYHOUND ACTION
Greyhound Action was formed in 1997 with the ultimate aim of putting an end to greyhound racing. There are many other groups which are dedicated to finding homes for ex-racing greyhounds, but in practical terms it is only possible to re-home a very small percentage of the vast number of greyhounds disposed of every year by the greyhound racing industry. Therefore the total abolition of greyhound racing is the only real solution. *Greyhound Action* is seeking to educate the public about the dark side of greyhound racing, so that support for this so-called "sport" withers away. We are also attempting to put pressure on the

government to ban greyhound racing altogether. We know it will take a long battle to achieve such a ban, but it is not an impossible aim, as the abolition of dog racing in several American states has shown.

As part of our campaign, a petition calling for a ban on greyhound racing has been produced, as well as leaflets, posters, badges, postcards and stickers. We also supply information to both local and national media and have been involved in campaigns (some of which have been successful) to stop the building of greyhound tracks both in this country and abroad and to end EU grants to Irish greyhound breeders. We are now putting considerable pressure on bookmakers to persuade them to no longer take bets on live greyhound racing and to switch to virtual (computerised) racing instead. In addition, we act as a central contact point for people who want to adopt ex-racing greyhounds and a considerable number of these dogs have found loving homes as a result.

Join our campaign by doing whatever you can to educate the public not to support greyhound racing. This can be done through street stalls, writing letters to newspapers and doing interviews in the local media. Demonstrations can be held outside greyhound tracks and leaflets distributed to those attending greyhound races and betting shops.

For more information please contact us.

Greyhound Action
PO Box 127
Kidderminster
DY10 3UZ
Tel: 01562 745778
Fax: 0870 138 3993
E-mail: info@greyhoundaction.org.uk
Website: www.greyhoundaction.org.uk

All the information above is either based on figures produced by the greyhound racing industry itself or on statements made by individuals who have worked either in the industry or in greyhound rescue.

Associations Who Have Helped With This Book

Thanks to all the wonderful people involved with campaigning for an end to greyhound racing, my request for contributions for this book went all over the world. I believe there are many groups and individuals who helped, by passing the message on, that I am not aware of, so I take this opportunity to thank you. If I have forgotten anyone who feels they should have got a mention, please accept my apologies, I really do appreciate your help.

Great Britain

Greyhound Action
www.greyhoundaction.co.uk
PO Box 127 Kidderminster DY10 3UZ
Tel: 01562 745778 Fax: 0870 1383993
Email: info@greyhoundaction.org.uk
For info of all their local branches please see their website.

Action For Greyhounds U.K
www.actionforgreyhoundsuk.org.uk
P.O. BOX 3089
Norwich,
Norfolk,
NR3 3YP
Tel: 01603 469864
Mobile: 07779 779015
Email: info@actionforgreyhoundsuk.org.uk

Greyhound Action Scotland
greyhoundactionscotland@btopenworld.com
www.greyhoundactionscotland.org.uk
07092 033640

Greyhound and Lurcher Rescue
www.greyhoundandlurcherrescue.co.uk

Tailends Rescue Centre
Telephone: +44 (0)1271 890689

Fax: +44 (0)1271 890130
Postal address:
Tailends
West Croyde
Croyde
Devon
England
EX33 1QA
E-mail: tailends@atlanticbreeze.co.uk

Greyhound Muses
www.greyhoundmuses.com
john11dogs@dogmail.com

East Anglia Animal Rights Coalition
PO Box 487, Norwich,
Norfolk, NR5 8WE
Telephone 07788 404 074
Email eastangliaarc@hotmail.com

Sheya Greyhound and Lurcher Rescue
www.sheyagreyhoundandlurcherrescue.com
Tel Julie Morgan on 0161 624 9176

Greyhound Compassion
www.hounddog.org.uk

Greyhound Gap
www.greyhoundgap.com

Give A Greyhound A Home
www.gagah.co.uk

Dogstrust
www.dogstrust.org.uk
Head Office
Dogs Trust
17 Wakley Street

London
EC1V 7RQ
020 7837 0006

Greyhounds and Golden Oldies,
Contact Diane Bostock on 01538 723505

Greyhound Gap
www.greyhoundgap.com/

Sighthound Welfare Trust
95 Celtic Crescent
Dorchester
Dorset
DT1 2TD
www.sighthoundwelfaretrust.org.uk
mail@sighthoundwelfaretrust.org.uk

Greyhound Rescue West of England
www.grwe.co.uk
07000 785092

Fen Bank Greyhound Sanctuary
The Farmhouse, Fen Bank , Friskney, Lincs PE22 8PS.
Tel: 01754 820593 or 01205 270166
www.fenbankgreyhounds.co.uk info@fenbankgreyhounds.co.uk

R.G.T Perry Barr
rgtperrybarr@blueyonder.co.uk.

Coventry Greyhound Group
www.coventrygroup.org.uk
email: admin@coventrygreyhound.org.uk

International

Scooby
C/O San Francisco n° 3
47400 Medina del Campo
(Valladolid)
España
Tel: +34 983 81 10 87
Fax: +34 983 83 75 79
www.scoobymedina.com
info@scoobymedina.com

Greyhound Protection International
http://www.greyhoundprotection.de/

Greyhound Protection League, America
P.O. Box 669 Penn Valley, CA 95946
www.greyhounds.org/

GREY2K USA
P.O. Box 442117
Somerville, MA 02144
Toll Free: 866-247-3925
Fax: 617-666-3568
Email: Info@GREY2KUSA.org

Greyhound Pets of America
www.greyhoundpets.org

Greyhound Ranch
http://www.petfinder.com/shelters/greyhoundranch.html

Galgos In Need, Denmark
www.galgo-sos.dk

Quick Order page

Have you enjoyed this book so much that you want copies for your friends? Perhaps a birthday present? Then fill in this order form and another copy will soon be on its way to you

U.K - Each book costs £8.75. plus postage and packing, at £1.25. Add £0.75 to the postage and packing cost for each additional book

U.S. - Each book costs $16 plus postage and packing, at $4.65 Add $2 to the postage and packing cost for each additional book

Europe - Each book costs 12.75 Euros plus postage and packing 2 Euros. Add 1 Euro to the postage and packing cost for each additional book

Two easy ways to pay:

Fill in the form below and then send a cheque, made payable to Helen Etheridge, to Grey's Publishing, Oakhurst, 4, Fifer's Lane, Old Catton, Norfolk. NR6 7AF. England

Name:

Address:

Email:

Number of copies:

Or, if you have a Paypal account, send me an email, at helenetheridge@ btinternet.com and I will invoice you through Paypal.

Thank you for purchasing "Greyhound Survivors." You have helped raise more money for Greyhound Action